W9-BUJ-528

400 CALORIES OR LESS WITH
OUR BEST BITES

2116

400 CALORIES OR LESS WITH
OUR BEST BITES

SARA WELLS • KATE JONES

SHADOW
MOUNTAIN

Photo inset on page iii, left to right: Steak and Green Bean Stir-Fry (p. 96), Angel Food Stacks with Lemon Cream and Fresh Berries (p. 126), Thai Chicken Salad (p. 42), Whole-Grain Waffles (p. 12)

All food styling and food photography by Sara Wells and Kate Jones
Art direction by Richard Erickson
Book and cover design by Sheryl Dickert Smith
Typography by Rachael Ward
Production design by Kayla Hackett

Visit us at ShadowMountain.com

Library of Congress Cataloging-in-Publication Data
Wells, Sara (Sara Smith), author.
  400 calories or less with our best bites / Sara Wells and Kate Jones.
    pages cm
  Other title: Four hundred calories or less with our best bites
  Includes index.
  Summary: A cookbook with recipes for dishes with less than 400 calories from the blog OurBestBites.com.
  ISBN 978-1-60907-991-8 (paperbound)
1. Cooking, American. 2. Low-calorie diet—Recipes. I. Jones, Kate (Kate Randle), author. II. Title. III. Title: Four hundred calories or less with our best bites.
  TX715.W4639 2015
  641.5973—dc23   2014039231

Printed in China
R. R. Donnelley, Shenzhen, China
10 9 8 7 6 5 4 3 2 1

CONTENTS

ACKNOWLEDGMENTS

First of all, we have to give a huge thank you to our readers, both those who have been with us from the very beginning and those who have just started reading *Our Best Bites* (and everyone in between). Thank you for your continued support, kindness, and friendship—without you, there would be no one to share our recipes and stories with.

Many thanks to our friends at Shadow Mountain for always supporting us as well as our creative vision. When we say we want a picture for every recipe, they find a way to make it happen.

Finally, thank you to our friends and families who have offered their endless support, advice, and taste-testing skills. Our husbands—Sam and Eric—and our kids—Clark, Meredith, and Will Jones, and Tyler, Owen, Jack, and Gavin Wells—have given us their unwavering patience (okay, mostly unwavering) and love. If we didn't have you behind us, following this particular dream would be impossible.

From our hearts and homes to yours,

Sara and Kate

Banh Mi Tacos, page 98

HOW TO USE THIS BOOK

At *Our Best Bites,* we wholeheartedly believe in eating delicious food. And when we're making a conscious effort to make better food choices, we still want our food to be tasty. We've thought about writing a book of lightened-up recipes for a long time, but our biggest hesitation was that there are a *lot* of different interpretations of what it means to eat healthy. There are people who believe low-fat is the only way to go, and others who subscribe to a low-carb way of life. There are paleo and low-calorie and gluten-free eaters. There are people who only make things from scratch and people who order frozen and dehydrated pre-cooked, pre-measured meals. Hop on the Internet and in about five minutes, you'll find twenty-five conflicting opinions on what "healthy" means.

We're not medical professionals or dietitians. We're just two girls who love good food and strongly believe in moderation. We've used these recipes to lose weight and to maintain healthy, balanced lifestyles ourselves. You'll find recipes in this book that fit into just about every category, but we do have a few important notes:

GLUTEN

We've labeled several recipes as gluten-free. Gluten is a combination of proteins found in certain foods, and while some people eat gluten-free because they just feel better not eating it, for others, their bodies can't process it and they become very sick when they eat even trace amounts of it. Sometimes gluten can show up in strange places, like some types of rice cereals but not in others, or in some brands of soy sauce but not others. If you are eating gluten-free or preparing a meal for someone who does not eat gluten, please be sure to check the labels on your ingredients, particularly for anything that is grain-based or may have some kind of grain-based flavor or coloring.

SODIUM

Due to the wide variances in sodium among different brands, we have not included a sodium calculation in the nutrition information, but it's easy to do by checking the nutritional information on the products you buy. Regardless of your sodium preferences, we recommend using low-sodium products and then seasoning to taste as necessary.

LOW CARB

Even in the low-carb world, there is some disagreement about what constitutes a low-carb recipe. If you are following a particular plan, you've probably been given numbers on what constitutes low carb, so feel free to use our numbers as a tool to help you determine whether or not the recipe will fit into your plan. Otherwise, any recipe with 20 grams of carbs or fewer per serving has been categorized as being low in carbs in this book.

WHITE VERSUS WHEAT

When it comes to calories, white and whole-grain breads, rice, and pastas are usually pretty comparable. That's not to say white is better—whole-grain breads, rice, and pastas are pretty much better in every way nutritionally—but let's face it, sometimes white just tastes better. In pretty much every recipe, white and whole-grain products can be used interchangeably, depending on your preference.

OUR WEIGHT LOSS PHILOSOPHY

As a general rule, we don't believe in cutting out entire food groups. We *do* believe that by maintaining an active lifestyle and eating lots of vegetables, fruits, and lean proteins, there's always room for a splurge, whether it's in the form of something sweet or a special occasion dinner. We've got calorie counts on every recipe—including delicious snacks and desserts—to help keep you where you want to be. We hope you'll use this book to find a healthy balance, whether you're trying to lose weight or stay balanced.

INTRODUCTION

When we started the *Our Best Bites* blog in 2008, we didn't anticipate it becoming what it is. We simply started out sharing our favorite recipes with our friends, sisters, aunts, and former roommates. And when we said, "our best bites," we meant "our best bites." You know—the recipes you make when your in-laws come for the weekend, when you really want to impress someone, when you're pulling out all the stops. Things like deep-fried French toast and stuffed pizza rolls and cheesy garlic bread rolls.

The funny thing is that those indulgences *aren't* all our best bites—they are special treats that we balance with fantastic-tasting lighter fare. We didn't realize there was some disconnect among our readers until people started telling us that they loved to read our blog and look at our pictures, but they couldn't eat what we were making because they were trying to eat healthy.

The truth is that we have always posted plenty of recipes that could easily fit into a healthy lifestyle, but many people didn't recognize them because they taste amazing. There's a common misconception that delicious food must be bad for you, or, on the flip side, that in order to lose weight, you can only eat steamed fish and vegetables. We wanted to show people that both of these ideas are faulty.

A balanced lifestyle has always been important to both of us. Like everyone else, there are times when we're better at balancing things than at other times, but generally speaking, we make great efforts to not only eat food that tastes amazing but is also good for us. After Sara lost fifty pounds, we realized that sharing these recipes is something that can help other people. This is real food that leads to a healthier lifestyle.

This book isn't about hiding vegetables or tricking your taste buds into thinking black beans are brownies. This is the real deal—tried and true food your family will eat, food you'll *want* to eat, whether you're actively trying to lose weight or if you're just making smart choices. We have more than sixty-five family-friendly recipes including meatless, low-carb, and gluten-free choices. There are recipes you could serve at dinner parties and recipes your kids will ask for again and again. And because we're big believers in balance in everything, we also have sweet treats and easy snacks to keep you on track no matter what.

Regardless of where you are in your journey towards a healthier lifestyle, we hope these recipes will help you like they've helped us. We can say with 100 percent certainty that even though there aren't recipes for deep-fried French toast, the things we're sharing in this cookbook are definitely Our Best Bites.

Nutrition

(for ½ cup quinoa, ¼ cup fresh berries,
½ tablespoon shredded coconut,
½ tablespoon toasted slivered
almonds, 2 tablespoons extra
coconut milk, and 1 teaspoon honey)

Calories: 194   **Fat:** 5.4g

Carbs: 31g   **Fiber:** 4g

Sugars: 13g   **Protein:** 5g

Add-On Options

• 8 ounces nonfat milk: 90 calories
• ½ navel orange: 40 calories
• ½ large grapefruit: 50 calories
• 1 slice whole-grain toast with
  2 teaspoons peanut butter: 163
  calories

Rollover Ingredient

coconut milk

COCONUT-ALMOND BREAKFAST QUINOA

MAKES 4 (½-CUP) SERVINGS

This sophisticated spin on breakfast cereal uses quinoa, a nutrient-rich superfood that cooks up incredibly creamy. It's similar enough to oatmeal that even picky eaters are likely to give it a shot!

½ cup quinoa, rinsed well and drained

1 cup coconut milk (from a carton, not a can)

2 teaspoons brown sugar

¼ teaspoon almond extract

TOPPINGS

Fresh berries

Shredded coconut, toasted if desired

Toasted slivered almonds

Additional coconut milk

Honey or agave syrup

1. Place rinsed and drained quinoa, coconut milk, brown sugar, and almond extract in a medium-sized pot. Stir ingredients and bring to a boil. Reduce heat to a simmer and cover pot, preferably with a clear lid, so you can see through it. Stir a few times during cooking. If mixture seems to be boiling out, crack the lid to release steam; otherwise, keep covered.

2. Cook for 10–15 minutes, until liquid is absorbed. In the last few minutes of cooking, feel free to add a little more liquid (water or additional coconut milk) until desired consistency is reached. A texture similar to oatmeal or porridge is ideal.

3. Divide quinoa into bowls and top with fresh berries, coconut and toasted almonds, and a splash of additional coconut milk. If desired, add a drizzle of honey or agave.

Nutrition

Calories: 292   **Fat:** 13g

Carbs: 23g   **Fiber:** 3g

Sugars: 3g   **Protein:** 22g

Add-On Options

- 1 cup mixed berries (strawberries, blueberries, raspberries): 70 calories
- 2 small wedges cantaloupe: 40 calories

Alternatives

Twelve slices of precooked bacon contain 36 calories, 4 grams of fat, and 2 grams of protein per serving.

Rollover Ingredient

chives

Author's Note

This is my all-time favorite go-to recipe when I'm short on time or don't know what to make for dinner. In fact, I keep a package of English muffins in my freezer for this very meal. Best of all, my kids will happily eat every bite!—*Kate*

ENGLISH MUFFIN BREAKFAST PIZZAS

MAKES 12 PIZZAS, OR 6 SERVINGS

Instead of topping these breakfast pizzas with cooked eggs, soak the English muffins in the egg mixture first (like savory French toast) and then top with your favorite omelet toppings: smoky ham, melted cheddar, green onions, mushrooms, tomatoes, etc. Best of all, they can be made in just a few minutes and served with fresh fruit for a quick breakfast or breakfast for dinner.

4 eggs, room temperature

2 tablespoons 1% milk

¼ teaspoon kosher salt

About 10 dashes Tabasco sauce

6 whole wheat English muffins, room temperature

12 thin slices deli ham (or precooked bacon)

Chopped vegetables, such as green onions, tomatoes, sliced olives, mushrooms, green peppers, chives, etc.

1 cup shredded cheddar or pepper Jack cheese

1. Preheat oven to 400 degrees F. Line a baking sheet with aluminum foil and spray liberally with nonstick cooking spray. Set aside.

2. In a pie plate, whisk together the eggs, milk, salt, and Tabasco sauce. If English muffins are not pre-sliced, cut each muffin in half. Otherwise, gently pull apart each muffin in half and soak each side in the egg mixture. You want the egg mixture to soak into the bread, but you don't want the English muffin to be falling apart. Place the muffin, cut side up, on the baking sheet.

3. If using ham, slice the ham into thin strips and place on top of the English muffins. If using bacon, crumble the cooked bacon and sprinkle it on top. Add additional desired toppings and then sprinkle with shredded cheese.

4. Bake 15 minutes and serve immediately.

   Freezer Instructions: After baking, loosen muffins from the baking sheet with a spatula and allow them to cool completely. Transfer the baking sheet to the freezer. When the pizzas are solid, transfer them to a large zip-top freezer bag. To reheat, place muffins on a microwave-safe plate and cook for 1½ minutes at a time until the pizza is heated through (actual time will vary depending on the microwave).

Nutrition

Calories: 254	Fat: 8g
Carbs: 30g	Fiber: 4g
Sugars: 3g	Protein: 14g

Alternatives

Substitute small corn tortillas if desired, and use queso fresco instead of feta.

Rollover Ingredients

cilantro, feta cheese, lime

Author's Note

This dish combines two of my family's favorite things: Latin food and breakfast for dinner. Eggs are such an easy source of protein and nutrients, and they combine beautifully with some of our favorite Latin flavors.—*Sara*

HUEVOS RANCHEROS INSPIRED EGGS

MAKES 6 SERVINGS

In rural Mexico, "rancher's eggs" are traditional mid-morning fare. Our version brings Latin-inspired flavors to your table for more than just breakfast. This filling egg dish makes a great lunch or dinner as well.

1 teaspoon olive oil

½ cup finely minced onion

2 cloves garlic, pressed or finely minced

1 jalapeño, seeds and membranes removed, finely minced

½ teaspoon ground cumin

¼ teaspoon kosher salt, more to taste

4–6 cracks freshly ground black pepper

1 (14.5-ounce) can fire-roasted tomatoes

6 small flour tortillas (6–8 inches)

6 eggs

1 (16-ounce) can low-fat refried beans, heated according to directions on can

6 tablespoons chopped cilantro

6 tablespoons reduced-fat feta cheese crumbles

6 lime wedges

1. Heat a medium-sized skillet over medium heat. When hot, add olive oil and then onion, garlic, and jalapeño. Sauté, stirring constantly, for 4–5 minutes. Add cumin, salt, and pepper. Stir.

2. Add tomatoes (including juices) and bring mixture to a simmer. Stir while simmering for about 5 minutes, using a spatula to scrape bottom of skillet to release browned vegetables. Set salsa mixture aside.

3. Heat a clean nonstick skillet and spray with nonstick cooking spray. Heat tortillas one at a time until bubbly and golden brown. Alternately, heat oven to 350 degrees F. and place a single layer of tortillas on a baking sheet. Bake 5–8 minutes, until warm and slightly toasted. Stack warmed tortillas on a plate and cover with foil to keep warm.

4. Spray the same skillet with nonstick cooking spray and crack eggs into the pan, spaced out evenly. Cover pan, place over medium-low heat, and cook until whites are set and yolks are still soft, about 3–5 minutes.

5. Spread ¼ cup beans on each tortilla and top with a fried egg. Spoon ¼ cup salsa over the top and sprinkle with 1 tablespoon each chopped cilantro and feta. Serve with lime wedges.

Nutrition

Calories: 192   **Fat:** 10g

Carbs: 1.5g   **Fiber:** 2g

Sugars: 6g   **Protein:** 15.8g

Add-On Options

- Side salad, see page 30
- 1 slice whole-grain bread with
  1 teaspoon butter: 143 calories
- ½ cup grapes: 52 calories

Shopping Tip

Look for precooked thinly sliced bacon in your grocery store. It heats up easily and quickly without a mess, and it's often lower in calories than other varieties of bacon.

Rollover Ingredient

chives

Author's Note

This is one of my favorite light dinners or lunches. Pair it with a side salad and a slice of whole-grain toast, and it's both filling and flavorful.—*Sara*

ROASTED TOMATO PARMESAN EGG CUPS

MAKES 6 SERVINGS

A creamy, savory custard is nestled in a delicate roasted tomato with hints of tangy onion and savory bacon. Topped with a layer of lightly browned Parmesan, this creative dish is as beautiful as it is delicious. Bake them together in a pan, or in individual ramekins for a fun twist.

6 medium-large, on-the-vine tomatoes

6 eggs

6 tablespoons low-fat cottage cheese

¾ cup freshly grated Parmesan cheese, divided

¾ teaspoon kosher salt

½ teaspoon freshly ground black pepper

¾ teaspoon garlic powder

4 tablespoons chopped fresh chives

2 slices bacon, cooked crisp (see Shopping Tip)

1. Preheat oven to 325 degrees F.

2. Use a sharp, serrated knife to cut off the top fourth of each tomato. Use a spoon to gently scoop out the loose inner contents of tomatoes, leaving the outside flesh intact. Use a knife to carefully remove larger pieces of flesh in the middle of the tomatoes. Lay cut-side down on several layers of paper towels and set aside.

3. Crack eggs into a medium-sized mixing bowl and lightly whisk. Add cottage cheese. Set aside 2 tablespoons of shredded Parmesan and add the remaining amount to the egg mixture. Also add salt, pepper, garlic powder, and chives. Whisk to combine.

4. Lightly spray a pie pan or individual ramekins with nonstick cooking spray. Gently shake any excess liquid from tomatoes and place them in pie pan or ramekin. Fill each tomato ¼-inch from top with egg mixture, and top each with about 1 teaspoon of reserved Parmesan. Crumble bacon and divide evenly between tomatoes.

5. Bake 50–55 minutes, until centers are puffed and golden and tops are slightly firm to the touch, but still have some give. Let rest 5–10 minutes before serving.

Nutrition

Calories: 202	**Fat:** 10g
Carbs: 4g	**Fiber:** 1g
Sugars: 2g	**Protein:** 20g

Add-On Options

- 1 slice whole-grain toast with 1 teaspoon butter: 143 calories
- 2 clementines: 70 calories
- ½ grapefruit: 50 calories
- 1 cup sliced strawberries: 53 calories

Author's Note

I love making egg dishes for a quick lunch while my kids are at school. It's a great (and fast!) way to get some protein while eating something grown-up, made just for me.—Sara

SPINACH ARTICHOKE OMELET

MAKES 1 SERVING

Spinach, artichokes, and Parmesan cheese are reminiscent of a decadent warm party dip, but they play out just as nicely in this good-for-you omelet. Keep a jar of marinated artichoke hearts in the fridge and make this several times during the week. It makes a great breakfast, lunch, or dinner!

1 whole egg

2 egg whites

1 tablespoon water

¼ teaspoon kosher salt

⅛ teaspoon freshly ground black pepper

⅛ teaspoon garlic powder

1 wedge low-fat soft cheese (such as Laughing Cow), regular or garlic herb

½ cup chopped fresh spinach leaves

2 marinated artichoke hearts, diced

2 tablespoons freshly grated Parmesan cheese

1. Heat an 8-inch nonstick frying pan to medium heat. Whisk together egg, egg whites, water, salt, pepper, and garlic powder.

2. Spray pan with nonstick cooking spray. Immediately add egg mixture and swirl to coat bottom of pan. Use a rubber spatula to gently scrape from the outside edge of the omelet inward, letting runny eggs flow to open spaces on bottom of pan, moving around the pan several times.

3. Cover the pan and turn heat to medium-low. Cook until top of omelet is almost set, about 2 minutes. Drop small dollops of the soft cheese on top, along with 1 tablespoon of Parmesan. Add chopped spinach, artichoke hearts, and the remaining Parmesan cheese.

4. Cover pan again and cook until top is set and cheese is melted. Slide onto serving plate either folded over or open-faced.

Nutrition

(for ½ round or 2 wedges from an 8-inch waffle iron)

Calories: 188   Fat: 11g

Carbs: 18g   Fiber: 3g

Sugars: 3g   Protein: 6g

Add-On Options

• 2 tablespoons berry-flavored Greek yogurt, ¼ cup fresh berries, ½ tablespoon honey: 70 calories

• *Cinnamon Apples*

In a medium-sized pan, sauté ⅓ cup diced apple with ½ teaspoon brown sugar, dash of cinnamon, and spritz of cooking spray, until softened. Top waffles with 2 tablespoons whipped cream from a can, ½ tablespoon maple syrup, and 1½ teaspoons toasted pecans: 100 calories

• 2 teaspoons peanut butter, 6 slices banana, ½ tablespoon honey, and dash of cinnamon: 120 calories

Alternatives

May substitute 4 tablespoons flour (whole wheat or all-purpose) in place of the wheat germ and flaxseed meal.

Shopping Tip

Wheat germ and flaxseed meal add nutrients, protein, and fiber. You can often find them in stores that sell bulk ingredients or near the health food section in the grocery store. You will need just a little for this recipe, but they will keep in the freezer.

WHOLE-GRAIN WAFFLES

MAKES 4 (8-INCH) WAFFLES; SERVING SIZE IS 2 WAFFLE WEDGES

These hearty, filling waffles are packed with nutrient-rich ingredients, but remain family friendly. Pile on some of our add-on options like peanut butter bananas or cinnamon apples and whipped cream for a specialty waffle. Prep a batch ahead of time and keep in the freezer for a wholesome breakfast on busy school mornings.

1½ cups whole wheat flour	½ teaspoon salt
¼ cup wheat germ	1½ cups nonfat milk
2 tablespoons ground flaxseed meal	⅓ cup canola oil
2 teaspoons baking powder	1 egg
2 tablespoons sugar	1 teaspoon vanilla

1. Whisk together flour, wheat germ, flaxseed meal, baking powder, sugar, and salt. In a separate bowl, mix together milk, oil, egg, and vanilla and whisk until combined. Add wet ingredients to dry and whisk until just mixed together. It's okay to have a few lumps; just don't overmix.

2. Ladle batter into an electric waffle iron and cook according to your waffle-maker's instructions until golden brown. Serve warm with desired toppings.

   Freezer Instructions: After cooking, lay waffles in a single layer on a baking dish. Place in the freezer for a few hours. When frozen, place in a zip-top bag or freezer container. Reheat in toaster. You can also keep cooled waffles in fridge and reheat in toaster.

Nutrition

Calories: 231   Fat: 3g

Carbs: 33g   Fiber: 9g

Sugars: 7g   Protein: 20g

Add-On Options

- 1 tablespoon light sour cream:
  20 calories
- 2 (¼-inch) slices) avocado: 50 calories
- 1 tablespoon grated Jack cheese:
  28 calories

Alternatives

Feel free to divide the recipe in half for a smaller batch. While we love the flavor intensity from a long, slow cook, feel free to simmer on the stove top instead, until sweet potatoes are tender.

Rollover Ingredients

cilantro, lime, sour cream

Author's Note

This chili feeds an army, so make sure you have a large slow cooker! The great news is that it freezes beautifully, so eat it one night for dinner, and then save the rest for a quick-fix meal another night.—Sara

BLACK BEAN AND SWEET POTATO TURKEY CHILI

MAKES 4 QUARTS, OR 10 (1½-CUP) SERVINGS

Don't be intimidated by some of the unique ingredients in this hearty chili. It has become a favorite among our blog readers. Packed with healthy ingredients and boasting hints of autumn flavors, this comforting meal is perfect for crisp fall nights.

1 tablespoon olive oil, divided

1 medium onion, diced

4 cloves garlic, peeled and minced

1 red bell pepper, diced

1–2 jalapeños, minced

20 ounces ground turkey breast

8 ounces mushrooms, minced (about 2 cups)

2 teaspoons ground cumin

2 teaspoons kosher salt

½ teaspoon ground black pepper

1 teaspoon oregano

1 teaspoon chili powder

1½ teaspoons smoked paprika

1½ pounds sweet potatoes, peeled and diced into ½-inch cubes

1 (28-ounce) can diced tomatoes, undrained

2 (15-ounce) cans black beans, drained and rinsed

1 (32-ounce) container beef broth

1 (15-ounce) can pumpkin puree

½ teaspoon cinnamon

1 tablespoon unsweetened cocoa powder

For serving: chopped cilantro, green onions, lime wedges

Sour cream (optional)

Sliced avocado (optional)

1. Heat a large skillet to medium-high heat. Add 1½ teaspoons olive oil and add onion, garlic, bell pepper, and jalapeños. Sauté about 5 minutes, until vegetables are tender and fragrant. Place in a slow cooker.

2. In the same skillet, heat remaining 1½ teaspoons olive oil. Add turkey and mushrooms and stir to combine. Sprinkle in cumin, salt, pepper, oregano, chili powder, and smoked paprika. Sauté, stirring frequently, until turkey is no longer pink. Add turkey mixture to slow cooker.

3. Add sweet potatoes, tomatoes, beans, beef broth, pumpkin, cinnamon, and cocoa powder to slow cooker and stir to combine. Cover and cook 4–6 hours on high, or 8–10 hours on low. Slow

cookers vary in temperature and cooking times so continue cooking until sweet potatoes are tender.

4. When done, turn off heat, uncover chili, and let it sit 10–15 minutes to thicken. Season with additional salt and pepper to taste before serving. Top each serving with desired amount of chopped cilantro, sliced green onions, and a squeeze of fresh lime juice. If desired, serve with sour cream and sliced avocados on top.

Nutrition

(1 cup soup with 1 tablespoon sliced green onion and 2 teaspoons yogurt)

Calories: 72   **Fat:** 2g

Carbs: 11g   **Fiber:** 2g

Sugars: 6g   **Protein:** 3g

Add-On Options

• *Grilled Cheese Half-Sandwich*

Layer ½ ounce Swiss cheese over 1 slice whole-grain bread. Spray hot skillet with nonstick cooking spray. Toast sandwich until cheese melts: 165 calories

• Side salad, see page 30

Alternatives

Substitute chicken broth in place of vegetable broth.

Cooking Tip

To drizzle yogurt, simply add water by teaspoonful to remaining yogurt in container, whisking until desired consistency is reached.

Rollover Ingredients

ginger, green onions, plain Greek yogurt

CARROT GINGER SOUP

MAKES 6 (1-CUP) SERVINGS

This light soup makes a great starter before a meal or a savory accompaniment to your favorite sandwich. Try it as an appetizer to help you feel full and get in a serving of vegetables before dinner even starts!

8–10 medium carrots (about 20 ounces)

2 medium tomatoes

2 teaspoons extra-virgin olive oil

2 cups diced onion

4 cloves garlic

1 tablespoon minced fresh ginger

1 (32-ounce) package vegetable broth

½ cup water

1½ teaspoons kosher salt

¼ teaspoon ground black pepper

1 (5.3-ounce) container nonfat Greek yogurt, divided (about ½ cup)

6 tablespoons sliced green onions

1. Remove ends from carrots and wash well. Slice into ½–1-inch pieces. Slice tomatoes in half. Remove seeds and pulp from each half and then cut into large chunks. Set aside.

2. Heat a large stockpot to medium heat. Add olive oil and onions and cook for 2–3 minutes, stirring often. Add garlic and ginger and sauté for an additional 30 seconds, until fragrant. Add carrots, tomatoes, vegetable broth, water, salt, and pepper. Bring soup to a boil and then reduce to a simmer. Cover pot and simmer 40–45 minutes, or until carrots are tender and easily broken with a fork.

3. Very carefully transfer soup to a blender. Remove stopper from blender lid to let steam escape, and hold a clean towel over hole. Process until soup is very smooth. Add ¼ cup yogurt and pulse to combine.

4. Return soup to pot and add additional salt to taste. Place servings in bowls and top each one with 1 tablespoon sliced green onion and about 2 teaspoons yogurt.

Nutrition

Calories: 272	Fat: 7g
Carbs: 33g	Fiber: 4g
Sugars: 8g	Protein: 18g

Add-On Options

- 2 tablespoons shredded sharp cheddar cheese or pepper Jack: 58 calories
- Small (2x2-inch) dinner roll: 80 calories
- Side salad, see page 30

Cooking Tip

If you live at a low elevation, check potatoes for doneness after 20 minutes.

Alternatives

We use leftover chicken from the Roasted Garlic-Lime Chipotle Chicken on page 74 to reduce preparation time.

Rollover Ingredient

chipotle chilies

CHIPOTLE CHICKEN CORN CHOWDER

MAKES 10 (1⅓-CUP) SERVINGS

This thick and hearty soup has a little bit of everything—smoky chipotle, black beans, sweet corn, baby potatoes, and tender bites of chicken. It's perfect for a cool fall or winter night!

4 tablespoons butter

1 large onion, minced

6–7 cloves garlic, minced

2 red, yellow, or orange bell peppers, chopped

1 chipotle chili, chopped (seeded to reduce heat)

½ heaping cup all-purpose flour

3 cups chicken broth

5 cups 1% milk

3 small red potatoes, chopped (about 8–10 ounces, cut into ½-inch cubes)

8 ounces skinless rotisserie chicken breast, chopped (about 2 cups)

1 cup frozen corn

1 (14.5 ounce) can black beans, drained and rinsed

2–3 teaspoons adobo sauce from canned chipotle chilies, to taste

1 teaspoon kosher salt

Chipotle hot sauce, to taste (like Tabasco)

1. Melt butter in a large pot over medium heat. Sauté onion, garlic, bell peppers, and chipotle chili until the vegetables are tender.

2. Reduce heat and add the flour. Cook 2–3 minutes. Add broth and cook until flour is smooth and broth is starting to thicken. Add milk and bring to a low simmer. You may need to increase heat to medium-low or medium.

3. Add potatoes and simmer for 30–35 minutes or until tender, stirring occasionally to make sure milk isn't burning. Add chicken, corn, black beans, and a small amount of adobo sauce a teaspoon at a time, and any additional salt to taste. If you'd like, add more chicken broth after cooking until desired consistency is reached. Serve with chipotle hot sauce.

Nutrition

Calories: 214	Fat: 6g
Carbs: 28g	Fiber: 2g
Sugars: 6g	Protein: 12g

Add-On Options

- Side salad, see page 30
- *Grilled Cheese Half-Sandwich*

  Layer ½ ounce cheese over 1 slice whole-grain bread. Spray hot skillet with nonstick cooking spray. Toast sandwich until cheese melts: 165 calories

Shopping Tips

- Look for both red curry paste (usually sold in small jars) and Udon noodles in the Asian and Thai aisle of the grocery store. If you can't find Udon noodles, substitute linguini, fettuccini, or spaghetti noodles.
- Refrigerated coconut milk in a carton has significantly fewer calories than even light canned coconut milk, averaging 80–90 calories per serving. While canned works better in some things, for the recipes in this book, we use coconut milk from a carton. Look for it near the regular milk. If desired, you can substitute canned light coconut milk.

Rollover Ingredients

cilantro, coconut milk, ginger, green onions, lime

COCONUT CURRY CHICKEN NOODLE SOUP

MAKES 6 (1½-CUP) SERVINGS

This revamped version of a classic feel-good soup boasts bold Thai flavors, but it is still just as homey and comforting as the original. Feel free to add or omit turmeric, which simply elevates the golden color of this beautiful soup.

2 teaspoons olive oil

3 stalks bok choy, or 6–8 stalks baby bok choy, white ends diced, and leafy greens set aside

1 cup diced onion

2 medium carrots, cut into 1-inch matchsticks

3 tablespoons minced fresh ginger

3 cloves garlic, minced

2 teaspoons red curry paste

1½ teaspoons curry powder

1 teaspoon kosher salt

1 (32-ounce) package low-sodium chicken broth

3½ cups coconut milk (from a carton)

2 cups water

1 teaspoon turmeric (optional)

6 ounces Japanese Udon noodles, broken into 1-inch pieces

2 cups diced or shredded cooked chicken breast

2–3 limes, divided

½ cup chopped cilantro

Sriracha hot sauce, to taste

½ cup sliced green onion

1. Heat a large stockpot to medium heat. Add olive oil and then diced white ends of bok choy, onion, and carrots. Cook 4–5 minutes, stirring often. Add ginger, garlic, red curry paste, curry powder, and salt. Stir for 30 seconds and then add chicken broth, coconut milk, water, and turmeric. Bring to a boil and then reduce to a simmer. Add noodles.

2. Cook until noodles are softened, 10–12 minutes. Add chicken. Dice leafy greens from bok choy and stir into soup until just wilted.

3. Remove from heat and add the juice from 1 lime, cilantro, and Sriracha hot sauce to taste. Garnish with green onions. Serve with additional lime wedges.

Nutrition

Calories: 256   Fat: 6g

Carbs: 24g   Fiber: 5g

Sugars: 15g   Protein: 24g

Add-On Options

- Small (2x2-inch) dinner roll: 80 calories
- Side salad, see page 30

Alternatives

Add your favorite vegetables including roasted squash, sautéed zucchini, or corn. Vegetables add negligible calories.

Cooking Tips

- Keep a bag of frozen vegetables in the fridge to speed up cooking time.
- An upright blender often works best to get this soup smooth and creamy. Use a ladle or measuring cup to transfer soup into blender, letting some broth remain in the pot. It's okay if you still have a few bits of cauliflower and onion remaining in the pot. That should allow you to blend the soup in one batch.

Author's Note

My kids love dipping grilled cheese sandwiches into this creamy, flavorful soup. They have no idea how many veggies Mom is sneaking into their tummies!—*Sara*

CREAMY CHICKEN AND VEGETABLE CHOWDER

MAKES 6 (1½-CUP) SERVINGS

This hearty chowder is comfort food at its best. If you love the flavors of a good pot pie but don't love the calories that come with it, fill up a bowl with this veggie-filled alternative. The cauliflower blends into a creamy base that will fool even the pickiest of eaters.

1½ teaspoons extra-virgin olive oil

2 cups diced onion

4–5 cloves garlic, chopped

4 cups chicken broth

6 cups chopped cauliflower

1½ teaspoons kosher salt

½ teaspoon ground black pepper

1 (12-ounce) can nonfat evaporated milk

1 (12-ounce) bag frozen mixed vegetables (carrots, peas, green beans)

12 ounces shredded cooked chicken breast (about 3 cups)

¾ cup freshly grated Parmesan cheese

1. Heat a large stockpot to medium heat. Add olive oil and onion. Sauté, stirring often, 2–3 minutes, until softened. Add garlic and sauté for 30 seconds more, until fragrant.

2. Add chicken broth, cauliflower, salt, and pepper. Bring to a boil and then reduce to a simmer. Cover with lid and simmer about 10 minutes, until cauliflower is very tender and easily sliced with a fork.

3. Remove pot from heat. Either use an immersion blender, or transfer mixture to an upright blender, in batches, if necessary for size constraints. Cover upright blender with lid and remove lid stopper to let steam escape. Cover hole with a clean towel and process soup in blender until completely smooth. (Always practice caution when blending hot liquids.)

4. Return mixture to pot and turn to medium heat. Add evaporated milk and vegetables. Bring to a low simmer. Add chicken and stir to heat through. Remove pot from heat and stir in cheese.

Nutrition

Calories: 218 **Fat:** 10g

Carbs: 23g **Fiber:** 2g

Sugars: 4g **Protein:** 14g

Add-On Options

• 2 (1-inch) slices French baguette: 140 calories

• Side salad, see page 30

Rollover Ingredient

low-fat cream cheese

CREAMY ITALIAN SAUSAGE AND POTATO SOUP

MAKES 10 (1½-CUP) SERVINGS

This creamy soup is loaded with Italian sausage and tender baby potatoes. It tastes like something you might find in a restaurant, and you won't even notice it's lightened up. Serve it with crusty whole wheat bread and a side salad to round out the meal.

20 ounces lean Italian turkey sausage links

½ teaspoon crushed red pepper flakes, plus more to taste

1 teaspoon smoked paprika

1 large onion, diced

5–6 cloves garlic, minced or pressed

6 cups chicken broth

1 teaspoon Italian seasoning

1½ pounds red potatoes, diced

2 cups 1% milk

3 ounces low-fat cream cheese

3 tablespoons all-purpose flour

½ teaspoon kosher salt

2 tablespoons butter

3 cups baby kale, chopped

½ cup plus 2 tablespoons freshly grated Parmesan cheese

1. Remove sausage from casings and crumble it into a large stockpot. Cook over medium heat and add red pepper flakes, smoked paprika, onion, and garlic. Sauté until the sausage is fully cooked. Drain if necessary.

2. Add the chicken broth and Italian seasoning, increase heat to high, and bring to a boil. Add diced potatoes. Cover pot, and reduce to a simmer. Cook potatoes until tender.

3. While the potatoes are cooking, place milk, cream cheese, flour, and salt in a blender. Blend until smooth.

4. In a small saucepan, heat butter over medium-low heat, then add the milk mixture and cook over medium heat until thick. (It should resemble a thick cream soup or pudding.)

5. When the potatoes are cooked, add the thickened milk mixture and chopped baby kale to the stockpot. Season with additional crushed red pepper flakes and kosher salt to taste. Top each serving with 1 tablespoon freshly grated Parmesan cheese.

Nutrition

Calories: 91   Fat: 4g

Carbs: 12g   Fiber: 4g

Sugars: 6g   Protein: 2g

Add-On Options

• *Half Turkey Sandwich*

1 slice whole-grain bread, 2 tea-spoons light mayo, lettuce leaves, 2 slices tomato, 2 ounces sliced turkey breast: 230 calories

Author's Note

Growing up in Logan, Utah, my family loved steaming bowls of canned cream of tomato soup on snowy winter days. Even though this version doesn't come from a can, it's delicious and still brings back those warm, comforting memories.—*Kate*

ROASTED RED PEPPER SOUP

MAKES 8 (1⅓-CUP) SERVINGS

This satisfying soup tastes rich (thanks to a bit of heavy cream) but is heavy on vegetables and light on calories. Sip a mug of it on a chilly afternoon or serve it with your favorite sandwich. It's the perfect comfort food.

4 large red bell peppers, seeded and cut into quarters

12 cloves garlic, peeled

2 cups cauliflower florets, broken into bite-sized pieces

1 large sweet onion, quartered

10 ounces grape tomatoes

¼ cup extra-virgin olive oil

1 teaspoon kosher salt, plus more to taste

¼ teaspoon freshly ground black pepper, plus more to taste

6 cups vegetable broth

2 tablespoons heavy cream

1. Preheat oven to 450 degrees F. Line a baking sheet with aluminum foil.

2. Place the quartered peppers, garlic, cauliflower, quartered onion, and grape tomatoes on the baking sheet. Drizzle with olive oil. Use your hands to toss the vegetables to coat them evenly with oil.

3. Sprinkle with salt and pepper and roast 35–40 minutes or until tomatoes are bursting, garlic is fragrant, onions are tender, and peppers are starting to blacken. Remove from oven and carefully transfer roasted vegetables to a large stockpot or Dutch oven.

4. Add the vegetable broth to the roasted vegetable mix and use an immersion blender to blend until completely smooth. Bring the soup just to a boil, then remove from heat. Add the heavy cream. Salt and pepper to taste.

Nutrition

(without Parmesan cheese)

Calories: 234   Fat: 6g

Carbs: 27g   Fiber: 2g

Sugars: 8g   Protein: 16g

Add-On Options

- Side salad, see page 30
- *Garlic Bread*

  1 slice whole wheat bread with 1½ teaspoons butter, 2 teaspoons crumbled Parmesan cheese, and garlic bread seasoning to taste. Broil until golden brown: 180 calories

Cooking Tip

If you want to up the vegetable quotient, add 1 cup of chopped mushrooms when you add the broth and tomatoes and then add a 10-ounce bag of fresh baby spinach during the last few minutes of cooking.

Rollover Ingredient

basil

SPAGHETTI SOUP

MAKES 8 (1½-CUP) SERVINGS

Both kids and adults love this no-frills soup that is perfect for picky eaters. Serve it with a tossed green salad and, if you'd like, a loaf of hot garlic bread.

1 tablespoon extra-virgin olive oil

1 pound 93% lean ground beef

1 large onion, diced (about 2 cups)

6 cloves garlic, minced

1 quart beef broth

2 (14.5-ounce) cans Italian-style diced tomatoes with basil and garlic

1 (15-ounce) can tomato sauce

1 teaspoon red wine vinegar

1 tablespoon Italian seasoning

1 tablespoon sugar

¼ teaspoon red pepper flakes

Kosher salt, to taste

Freshly ground black pepper, to taste

6 ounces spaghetti, broken into fourths

½ cup freshly grated Parmesan cheese (optional)

Chopped fresh basil (optional)

1. Heat the olive oil in a large pot over medium-high heat. When hot, add the ground beef, onion, and garlic. Cook until the ground beef is browned and the onions are tender and fragrant.

2. Add the remaining ingredients except spaghetti, Parmesan cheese, and basil and bring to a boil over high heat. Add broken spaghetti and cook until pasta is al dente. Top each bowl with 1 tablespoon freshly grated Parmesan cheese, if desired. Serve immediately.

   Leftovers can be served as a delicious all-in-one spaghetti with meat sauce.

THE SALAD BAR

Have you ever eaten out at a restaurant and thought you were making the smart choice by ordering a salad, then you come home and look it up and realize that your healthy salad had something like 1,100 calories and 72 grams of fat? We've been there.

A big, fresh salad can make a perfect meal, and it's easy when your refrigerator and pantry are stocked with a variety of ingredients. Use this guide to craft the perfect salad and know exactly what you're eating!

BASIC SALAD DRESSING INSTRUCTIONS

A basic vinaigrette consists of a fat (oil) and an acid (vinegar or citrus). Those two elements alone, along with a sprinkle of kosher salt and freshly ground black pepper, make a perfect, simple dressing.

To customize your dressing even more, try starting with a ratio of two parts oil to one part vinegar (or citrus juice), then whisk in other flavors like mustard, fresh herbs, minced garlic, or dry seasonings.

For a creamy dressing, try whisking your flavoring agents into light mayonnaise, sour cream, or plain Greek yogurt.

FLAVOR COMBINATION IDEAS

Asian Slaw
Shredded cabbage or coleslaw mix, shredded, cooked chicken thigh meat, edamame, shredded carrots, sugar snap peas, mandarin oranges, Asian noodles, or chopped peanuts

Dressing: canola oil, rice vinegar, sesame oil, honey, soy sauce

Berry Chicken
Baby spinach leaves, chicken breast, strawberries, blueberries, raspberries, slivered almonds, diced avocado

Dressing: olive oil, red wine vinegar, honey, salt, and pepper

Chicken and Feta
Baby mixed greens, grilled chicken breast, crumbled feta cheese, purple grapes, red onion slices, sliced baby cucumber

Dressing: store-bought light balsamic vinaigrette

Classic Cobb
Iceberg lettuce, cooked chicken breast or ham, hard-boiled egg, tomatoes, red onion, avocado, crumbled blue cheese, crumbled bacon

Dressing: low-fat store-bought Ranch

Indian
Spinach, cooked chicken thigh meat, dried cherries, green onions, shredded carrots, cashews, garbanzo beans

Dressing: tahini, lemon juice, curry powder, salt, and pepper

Mediterranean
Romaine, thinly sliced cooked steak, cherry tomatoes, olives, marinated artichokes, cucumber, feta cheese

Dressing: olive oil, balsamic vinegar, salt, and pepper

Southwest
Romaine, roasted turkey breast, green onions, bell pepper, red onion, pepperoncini, black beans, queso fresco, croutons

Dressing: canola oil, lime juice, chili powder, cumin, salt, and pepper

Tropical
Mixed spring greens, grilled shrimp, mango, pineapple, green onions, quinoa

Dressing: canola oil, rice vinegar, honey, lemon juice, salt, and pepper

Greens	Qty	Cals	Fat (g)	Carbs (g)	Sugars (g)	Fiber (g)	Protein (g)
Arugula	2 cups	12	0	2	1	1	1
Mixed spring greens	2 cups	13	0	2	0	1	1
Fresh spinach	2 cups	14	0	2	0	2	2
Romain lettuce, chopped	2 cups	15	0	2	2	2	2
Iceberg lettuce, shredded	2 cups	20	0	4	2	2	2
Bagged coleslaw mix	2 cups	27	0	7	4	3	1
Shredded cabbage	2 cups	34	0	4	4	4	2
Broccoli slaw	2 cups	50	0	10	4	4	2
Kale, chopped	2 cups	66	0	12	0	2	5

Proteins (weight after cooking)	Qty	Cal	Fat (g)	Carbs (g)	Sugars (g)	Fiber (g)	Protein (g)
Bacon, crumbled or chopped	1 slice	43	3	0	0	0	3
Ham, diced	¼ cup	62	3	0	0	0	8
Hard-boiled egg, large	1 egg	70	5	0	0	0	6
Tuna (canned white chunk)	3 ounces	80	1	0	0	0	16
Shrimp	3 ounces	84	1	0	0	0	18
Roasted turkey breast	3 ounces	87	0	3	3	0	15
Boneless skinless chicken breast	3 ounces	96	2	0	0	0	20
Chicken thigh meat	3 ounces	102	5	0	0	0	14
Sliced lean steak (like flank)	3 ounces	156	6	0	0	0	24
Roasted turkey, dark meat	3 ounces	165	7	0	0	0	24
Salmon, fillet	3 ounces	175	10	0	0	0	19

Dairy	Qty	Cals	Fat (g)	Carbs (g)	Sugars (g)	Fiber (g)	Protein (g)
Cottage Cheese (2%)	1 tablespoon	12	0	0.5	0.5	0	2
Feta cheese, crumbled	1 tablespoon	16	1	0	0	0	1
Parmesan, shredded	1 tablespoon	20	1	0	0	0	2
Mozzarella (part skim), shredded	1 tablespoon	21	1	0	0	0	2
Cotija or queso fresco, crumbled	1 tablespoon	23	2	0	0	0	2
Cheddar or Jack cheese, shredded	1 tablespoon	28	2	0	0	0	2
Blue cheese, crumbled	1 tablespoon	30	2	0	0	0	2
Fresh mozzarella, diced	2 tablespoons	30	2	0	0	0	3
Gorgonzola, crumbled	1 tablespoon	50	4	0	0	0	3

Fruits	Qty	Cals	Fat (g)	Carbs (g)	Sugars (g)	Fiber (g)	Protein (g)
Mandarin oranges, canned, drained	¼ cup	10	0	2	2	0	0
Raspberries	¼ cup	13	0	4	1	2	0
Strawberries, sliced	¼ cup	14	0	3	3	1	0
Apples, with skin, diced	¼ cup	14	0	4	3	1	0
Navel oranges, medium	3 segments	15	0	4	3	1	0
Pineapple, diced	¼ cup	20	0	6	4	0.5	0
Blueberries	¼ cup	21	0	5	4	1	0
Grapefruit, diced sections	¼ cup	24	0	6	4	1	0.5
Mango, diced	¼ cup	27	0	7	8	2	0
Peaches, sliced	½ cup	30	0	8	6	1	0.5
Nectarines, sliced	½ cup	32	0	8	6	1	1
Grapes, red or green seedless	10 grapes	34	0	9	8	0	0
Plums, sliced	½ cup	38	0	10	8	1	0.5
Pears, sliced	½ cup	40	0	11	7	2	0.5
Avocado, cubes	¼ cup	60	6	0	0	3	1
Dried cranberries	2 tablespoons	65	0	17	15	2	0
Dried cherries	2 tablespoons	65	0	16	14	0.5	0.5

Vegetables	Qty	Cals	Fat (g)	Carbs (g)	Sugars (g)	Fiber (g)	Protein (g)
Green onions, chopped	1 tablespoon	1	0	0	0	0	0
Celery, diced	¼ cup	4	0	1	0.5	0.5	0
Mushrooms, sliced	¼ cup	4	0	0.5	0	0	0.5
Pepperoncini, sliced	2 tablespoons	5	0	1	0	0	0
Tomato, cherry	¼ cup	7	0	2	1	1	0
Cucumber, sliced	½ cup	8	0	2	1	0	0
Shredded carrots	¼ cup	11	0	3	1	1	0
Bell peppers, diced	¼ cup	12	0	1	2	1	0
Red onion slices	5 rings	12	0	3	1	0	0
Broccoli, raw, chopped	½ cup	15	0	3	1	1	1
Marinated artichoke hearts, jarred	3 hearts	30	3	3	0	2	0
Black olives, medium	8 olives	32	0	0	0	0	0
Sugar snap peas, whole	10 pea pods	42	0	8	4	3	3

Crunchy Toppings	Qty	Cals	Fat (g)	Carbs (g)	Sugars (g)	Fiber (g)	Protein (g)
Croutons	¼ cup	30	0.5	6	0	0.5	1
Asian noodles, crunchy	2 tablespoons	30	1	1	0	0	0
Sunflower seeds	1 tablespoon	37	3	1	0	1	1
Slivered almonds	1 tablespoon	39	3	1	0	1	1
Chopped cashews	1 tablespoon	40	3	2	0	0	1
Chopped peanuts	1 tablespoon	53	5	2	0	1	2

Beans and Grains	Qty	Cals	Fat (g)	Carbs (g)	Sugars (g)	Fiber (g)	Protein (g)
Pinto beans	2 tablespoons	26	0	5	0	1	2
Kidney beans, canned, drained	2 tablespoons	27	0	5	0.5	2	2
Quinoa, cooked	2 tablespoons	28	0.5	5	0	0.5	1
Black beans, canned, drained	2 tablespoons	29	0	5	0	2	2
Edamame, shelled	2 tablespoons	30	1	2	0.5	1	2
Garbanzo beans, canned, drained	2 tablespoons	36	0	7	0	1	1
Navy beans, canned, drained	2 tablespoons	37	0	7	0	2	3
Great Northern beans, canned, drained	2 tablespoons	37	0	7	0	2	2

Condiments for Dressings	Qty	Cals	Fat (g)	Carbs (g)	Sugars (g)	Fiber (g)	Protein (g)
Other vinegars	1 tablespoon	3	0	0	0	0	0
Dijon mustard	1 teaspoon	4	0	0	0	0	0
Lime juice	1 tablespoon	4	0	1	0	0	0
Lemon juice	1 tablespoon	4	0	1	0	0	0
Greek yogurt, low fat	1 tablespoon	10	0	1	1	0	3
Soy sauce	1 teaspoon	11	0	1	0	0	2
Balsamic vinegar	1 tablespoon	14	0	3	2	0	0
Honey	1 teaspoon	20	0	6	5	0	0
Sour cream, light	1 tablespoon	20	1	1	1	0	1
Tahini	1 teaspoon	30	3	1	0	0	1
Light mayonnaise	1 tablespoon	35	4	1	0	0	0
Olive oil	1 teaspoon	40	5	0	0	0	0
Canola oil	1 teaspoon	40	5	0	0	0	0
Avacado oil	1 teaspoon	40	5	0	0	0	0
Grapeseed oil	1 teaspoon	40	5	0	0	0	0
Sesame oil	1 teaspoon	40	5	0	0	0	0

Nutrition

Calories: 245   **Fat:** 10g

Carbs: 29g   **Fiber:** 4g

Sugars: 5g   **Protein:** 13g

Alternatives

Feel free to substitute chicken broth for the vegetable broth. Lime juice would make a good substitution for lemon juice.

Cooking Tip

Prepare your quinoa and chicken the day before so they're nice and chilled to start with.

Rollover Ingredient

cilantro

CURRY CASHEW QUINOA SALAD

MAKES 6 (1-CUP) SERVINGS

Savory curried quinoa provides a flavorful backdrop for this tangy and filling salad. Complete with protein-packed chicken and cashews, fresh parsley or cilantro, and sweet ripe pineapple, this good-for-you salad will fill you up but keep you coming back for more!

1 cup dry quinoa

2 cups vegetable broth

2½ teaspoons curry powder, divided

Kosher salt

¾ cup diced fresh pineapple

⅓ cup diced red onion

⅓ cup fresh parsley or cilantro, chopped

1½ cups diced cooked chicken breast

½ cup chopped cashews

DRESSING

2 tablespoons olive oil

1 tablespoon honey

1 tablespoon rice vinegar

4 tablespoons freshly squeezed lemon juice

¼ teaspoon kosher salt

⅛ teaspoon ground black pepper

1. Place quinoa in a small bowl and cover with cool water. Soak for 5 minutes and then strain with a fine mesh strainer, rinsing well.

2. Bring vegetable broth to a boil in a medium-sized pot. Add 1½ teaspoons curry powder, drained quinoa, and a pinch of salt. Reduce heat to a simmer, cover, and cook until liquid has been absorbed, about 15 minutes. Set aside to cool, and then refrigerate until chilled.

3. Combine chilled quinoa, pineapple, onion, parsley or cilantro, and chicken. Gently toss to combine.

4. Make dressing by mixing olive oil, honey, vinegar, remaining 1 teaspoon curry powder, and lemon juice in a small jar. Add salt and pepper, and shake to combine.

5. Pour 5 tablespoons of dressing over quinoa mixture and gently toss to combine. Season with additional salt and pepper to taste. Right before serving, stir in cashews. Add additional dressing if desired.

Nutrition

Calories: 109   **Fat:** 5g

Carbs: 14g   **Fiber:** 2g

Sugars: 5g   **Protein:** 4g

Add-On Options

- 4 ounces grilled boneless, skinless chicken breast: 110 calories
- 3 ounces thinly sliced grilled flank steak: 156 calories
- 4 ounces cooked salmon filet: 170 calories
- 2 (1-inch) slices French baguette: 140 calories

Alternatives

This salad is best with fresh corn from the cob, but if corn is out of season, substitute thawed frozen. Avoid canned corn.

Rollover Ingredients

basil, feta cheese, green onions

Author's Note

We make this salad all summer long at my house, taking advantage of local sweet corn and ripe tomatoes straight from the garden.—*Sara*

FRESH CORN SALAD

MAKES 6 (¾-CUP) SERVINGS

The best of summer's flavors are highlighted in this fresh, light salad. Turn it into a main dish by adding a serving of grilled steak, chicken, or fish.

4 ears fresh corn, husks and silk removed

10 ounces grape tomatoes (about 2 cups)

1/3 cup sliced green onions

¼ cup chopped fresh basil

1½ tablespoons olive oil

¼ teaspoon minced garlic

2½ tablespoons red wine vinegar

½ teaspoon kosher salt

½ teaspoon freshly ground black pepper

½ cup crumbled reduced-fat feta cheese

Optional protein of your choice from the Add-On Options

1. Bring a large pot of water to a boil. Add corn and return to a boil, cooking for about 6–7 minutes. While corn is cooking, fill a large bowl or 9x13-inch baking dish with ice water. Use tongs to remove corn from pot and immediately plunge in ice water until cooled.

2. Use a sharp knife to remove corn kernels from cobs and place corn in a mixing bowl. Cut tomatoes in half and add them to the bowl along with the green onions and basil. Add olive oil, garlic, vinegar, salt, and pepper, and toss to coat.

3. Add feta and very gently toss salad to distribute cheese. Cover bowl and refrigerate for at least 1 hour, but for best results, chill 4–6 hours.

Nutrition

Calories: 243 **Fat:** 6g

Carbs: 26g **Fiber:** 6g

Sugars: 3g **Protein:** 25g

Alternatives

If you're watching your carbs, skip the pita and serve this salad on top of a larger portion of spinach.

Cooking Tip

If you can't find Greek herb seasoning, combine ½ teaspoon dried oregano, ¼ teaspoon dried basil, ¼ teaspoon dried mint, and a pinch of kosher salt.

Rollover Ingredients

green onions, feta cheese, plain Greek yogurt

GREEK CHICKEN SALAD PITAS

MAKES 4 SERVINGS

Tender roasted chicken, tangy Greek yogurt, and crisp cucumbers come together in this quick and easy chicken salad with a twist that's perfect for hot summer evenings.

8 ounces shredded rotisserie chicken breast (about 2 cups)

1 teaspoon lemon zest

1 teaspoon minced garlic

3 green onions, chopped

¼ cup crumbled feta cheese

½ cup plain fat-free yogurt

½ teaspoon red wine vinegar

¾ teaspoon Greek herb seasoning

½ cup grape tomatoes, halved

1 cup sliced, seeded cucumbers

Salt and pepper, to taste

1 cup baby spinach leaves

4 whole-grain pita pockets

1. In a medium bowl, toss together chicken breast, lemon zest, garlic, green onions, and feta cheese. Set aside.

2. In a small bowl, whisk together yogurt, red wine vinegar, and Greek herbs. Toss the dressing with the chicken mixture and refrigerate for at least 1 hour and up to several hours.

3. Right before serving, add the tomatoes and cucumbers. Season to taste with salt and pepper. Divide the spinach evenly among the pita pockets and then divide the chicken salad evenly. Serve immediately.

SINGLE SERVING RECIPE

2 ounces shredded rotisserie chicken breast (about 2 cups)

¼ teaspoon lemon zest

¼ teaspoon minced garlic

2 tablespoons green onions, chopped

2 tablespoons crumbled feta cheese

2 tablespoons plain fat-free yogurt

Dash red wine vinegar

¼ teaspoon Greek herb seasoning

3–4 grape tomatoes, halved

¼ cup sliced, seeded cucumbers

¼ cup baby spinach leaves

1 whole-grain pita pocket

Nutrition

(salad only)

Calories: 267   **Fat:** 12g

Carbs: 8g   **Fiber:** 2g

Sugars: 6g   **Protein:** 28g

Add-On Options

• 1 slice whole-grain bread (open-faced sandwich): 110 calories

• Whole-grain wrap or pita pocket: 100 calories

• 8 Wheat Thin crackers: 70 calories

• 1 rice cake: 50 calories

Alternatives

Feel free to add more curry powder and red wine vinegar to taste.

Rollover Ingredients

green onions, plain Greek yogurt, sour cream

Author's Note

When I'm working on weight-loss, this is one of my go-to lunches. I plan ahead when making dinner during the week, and just cook up a little extra chicken so I'll have some to make this the next day. A rotisserie chicken also works great, and you can make several servings at a time to eat throughout the week.—*Sara*

GUILTLESS CHICKEN SALAD

MAKES 1 SERVING

Traditional chicken salads are notoriously calorie-laden, but this lightened up version packs in both protein and flavor, and chances are you won't even know it's better for you. Perfectly portioned for one, it makes a great lunchtime solution. Make it ahead of time, as the flavor improves after a long chill in the fridge.

4 ounces cooked shredded or diced boneless, skinless, chicken breast (about 1 cup)

¼ cup diced celery

2 tablespoons sliced green onion

¼ cup diced apple

1 tablespoon light mayonnaise

1 tablespoon light sour cream or Greek yogurt

½–1 tablespoon chopped fresh parsley or cilantro (optional)

⅛ teaspoon curry powder

¼ teaspoon red wine vinegar

1 tablespoon toasted sliced almonds

Salt and pepper, to taste

In a large bowl, combine all ingredients except almonds and stir to combine. If possible, chill for 1 hour before eating. Before serving, mix in almonds. Eat in a lettuce wrap, on whole-grain bread, in a wrap, or in a pita.

Nutrition

Calories: 393   **Fat:** 17g

Carbs: 29g   **Fiber:** 4g

Sugars: 9g   **Protein:** 35g

Add-On Options

• Serve salad in a whole-grain wrap or pita pocket: 100 calories

Rollover Ingredients

cilantro, green onion, lime

THAI CHICKEN SALAD

MAKES 1 SERVING

Keep these ingredients on hand in the fridge, and a quick-fix lunch for one is minutes away. Whether you pack it for lunch at work or eat it on the run at home, this protein-packed dish will keep you full and satisfied for hours.

1 cup coleslaw cabbage mix

4 ounces cooked, shredded chicken (about 1 cup)

⅓ cup cooked quinoa, cooled

1 green onion, chopped

¼ cup shelled edamame

2 tablespoons chopped cilantro

¼ cup diced cucumber or celery

1 tablespoon chopped cashews or peanuts

DRESSING

1 teaspoon creamy peanut butter

1 teaspoon honey

1 teaspoon olive oil

1 tablespoon rice vinegar

1 teaspoon low sodium soy sauce

Lime wedge (optional)

1. In a large bowl, combine cabbage, chicken, quinoa, onion, edamame, cilantro, and cucumber.

2. In a small bowl, whisk peanut butter and honey together. Whisk in oil, and then vinegar and soy sauce. Toss dressing with salad.

3. Top with chopped nuts and serve with a squeeze of lime juice.

Nutrition

Calories: 66   Fat: 2g

Carbs: 10g   Fiber: 3g

Sugars: 0g   Protein: 3g

Rollover Ingredient

rosemary

ARTICHOKE WHITE BEAN DIP

MAKES 16 (2 TABLESPOON) SERVINGS

This savory dip has hints of Italian flavors and is delicious served with pita or pretzel chips, carrot sticks, or as a spread on sandwiches or bagels.

2 cans Great Northern beans, drained and rinsed

1 (14-ounce) jar marinated artichoke hearts, drained

4 cloves garlic

Juice of 1 lemon

2 tablespoons plus 1 teaspoon extra-virgin olive oil

Salt and pepper, to taste

1 tablespoon chopped fresh rosemary leaves (optional)

1. Place beans, artichoke hearts, garlic, lemon juice, and 2 tablespoons olive oil in blender and blend until smooth. If necessary, add more oil to reach desired consistency.

2. Season to taste with salt and pepper and transfer to a serving dish. Allow to stand for at least 30 minutes.

3. Before serving, drizzle with 1 teaspoon olive oil and garnish with a pinch of coarse salt and freshly cracked pepper and, if desired, chopped rosemary leaves. Refrigerate until ready to serve. Serve with fresh vegetables, freshly baked bread, pita chips, pretzel chips, as a spread on sandwiches, or on salads.

Nutrition

Calories: 85   **Fat:** 6g

Carbs: 4g   **Fiber:** 2g

Sugars: 0g   **Protein:** 4g

Shopping Tip

Look for bags of shelled edamame, which are the small beans already removed from their pods, in the freezer section of the grocery store.

EDAMAME HUMMUS

MAKES 6 (¼-CUP) SERVINGS

Nutrient-rich edamame makes the base of this amazingly flavorful dip. Dunk pita chips, pretzels, or fresh vegetables in it, or use as a spread on sandwiches and wraps.

1¼ cups shelled edamame (about 8 ounces)

1½ tablespoons tahini

¾ teaspoon minced garlic

3 teaspoons extra-virgin olive oil, divided

1½–2 tablespoons lemon juice

¼ teaspoon kosher salt, plus more to taste

Black pepper

3–4 tablespoons water

3 tablespoons diced roasted red bell pepper

Toasted sesame seeds (plain or black)

1. Place edamame, tahini, garlic, 2 teaspoons olive oil, lemon juice, salt, and pepper in a food processor. Pulse several times, using a spatula to scrape down sides of food processor bowl.

2. Add water until mixture blends continuously in food processor and desired consistency is reached. Stop occasionally to scrape down sides of food processor bowl. Process for several minutes, until mostly smooth. Add additional salt and pepper to taste.

3. Transfer to a serving bowl and top with diced peppers. Drizzle with remaining 1 teaspoon olive oil and sprinkle with a few sesame seeds.

Nutrition

Calories: 48   Fat: 0g

Carbs: 13g   Fiber: 1g

Sugars: 12g   Protein: 0g

Cooking Tip

Baking time will depend on the thickness of your apple slices. Extra-thin slices from a mandolin will bake in about 7 hours, while thicker slices may take 8 or more.

Prep Tip

A mandolin is an ideal tool for perfectly thin, uniform slices. You can find them very reasonably priced at the store or online.

OVEN-BAKED CINNAMON APPLE CHIPS

MAKES 2 (½-OUNCE) SERVINGS

Oven drying takes time, but it produces very little heat and is a great project for a day when you're around the house anyway. These apple chips turn out crisp and sweet, making them the perfect snack. Instructions and nutritional information reflect just one apple, but take advantage of the space in your oven by multiplying the quantities and fitting in as many pans as possible!

1 large apple, cored   ⅛–¼ teaspoon ground cinnamon (optional)

1. Slice apple in uniformly thin slices (less than ⅛-inch) and place in an even layer on baking sheet lined with either parchment or a silicone baking mat. Slices can touch each other, but try not to overlap. Fit as many apples on a sheet as you can. (They shrink a lot!) If desired, sprinkle with cinnamon or gently rub cinnamon into surface of the apples.

2. Bake apples at 170 degrees F. for 7–8 hours, until dry and slightly shriveled. The edges should be curled up with a slight golden-brown hue. Without opening the oven, turn off heat. Leave oven door shut until completely cooled. Remove apples from baking sheet and store in an air-tight container.

Nutrition

(herbed garlic parmesan popcorn)

Calories: 199	Fat: 12g
Carbs: 14g	Fiber: 2g
Sugars: 0g	Protein: 9g

(chili-lime popcorn)

Calories: 124	Fat: 7g
Carbs: 13g	Fiber: 3g
Sugars: 0g	Protein: 2g

(cinnamon-brown sugar popcorn)

Calories: 137	Fat: 6g
Carbs: 19g	Fiber: 3g
Sugars: 6g	Protein: 2g

Cooking Tip

If you prefer microwave popcorn, look for plain or salt-only varieties. If you use a salted popcorn, omit salt from the ingredients and salt to taste before serving. Additionally, you'll need to adjust the calories and fat to account for oil used to pop the popcorn.

Rollover Ingredient

lime

POPCORN

MAKES 4 (2-CUP) SERVINGS

Popcorn is a great, satisfying whole-grain snack that can be salty or sweet (or both!) depending on your mood. Too often, it's weighed down by oil, butter, or sugar; and while those can be delicious, so are these lighter options!

HERBED GARLIC PARMESAN POPCORN

1 tablespoon butter

1 tablespoon extra-virgin olive oil

1 large clove garlic, pressed

¼ teaspoon dried thyme

¼ teaspoon dried basil

¼ teaspoon dried rosemary

8–10 cups air-popped popcorn (see Cooking Tip)

¾ cup finely grated Parmesan cheese, more if desired

3–4 cracks freshly ground black pepper

1. Place butter, olive oil, and garlic in a small saucepan over medium-low heat. Heat until butter melts and starts to lightly simmer. Stir with rubber spatula and cook 1–2 minutes, until garlic is softened and fragrant. Add thyme, basil, and rosemary, and stir to combine. Remove pan from heat and set aside.

2. Prepare popcorn and place in large mixing bowl. Drizzle butter mixture over popcorn while stirring with large spoon or spatula. Quickly toss to coat. Add Parmesan cheese and black pepper and toss until well distributed. Top with additional Parmesan if desired. Serve immediately.

CHILI-LIME POPCORN

8 cups air-popped popcorn (see Cooking Tip)

2 tablespoons extra-virgin olive oil

½ teaspoon chili powder

½ teaspoon garlic powder

½ teaspoon freshly grated lime zest

¼ teaspoon kosher salt (or to taste)

¼ teaspoon ground coriander

Place popped corn in a large bowl. In a small bowl, whisk together the remaining ingredients and drizzle over the popcorn. Toss immediately to coat popcorn evenly. Serve immediately.

CINNAMON-BROWN SUGAR POPCORN

8 cups air-popped popcorn (see Cooking Tip)

2 tablespoons unsalted butter, melted

2 tablespoons brown sugar

½ teaspoon ground cinnamon

Salt to taste

Place popped corn in a large bowl. In a small bowl, combine melted butter, brown sugar, and cinnamon. Whisk to combine completely. Drizzle over popcorn and quickly toss to coat popcorn evenly. Serve immediately.

Nutrition

Calories: 85   **Fat:** 4g

Carbs: 10g   **Fiber:** 3g

Sugars: 1g   **Protein:** 3g

Cooking Tip

Feel free to experiment with different spices and flavors of olive oil. Try to keep the spices between 1½–2 teaspoons with at least ½ teaspoon of salt. Chili powder, cumin, coriander, onion powder, rosemary, dehydrated lime and lemon—there are lots of possibilities!

ROASTED GARLIC CHICKPEAS

MAKES 6 (⅓-CUP) SERVINGS

This is a great little snack if you're craving something salty and crunchy! Pack individual portions for when you are hungry on-the-go.

1 (15-ounce) can chickpeas

1½ teaspoons extra-virgin olive oil

½ teaspoon kosher salt

¼ teaspoon freshly ground black pepper

¾ teaspoon garlic powder

½ teaspoon dry parsley

1. Preheat oven to 400 degrees F. Line a baking sheet with aluminum foil.

2. Drain and rinse chickpeas and pat dry with a paper towel. Transfer chickpeas to the prepared baking sheet.

3. In a small bowl, whisk together olive oil, salt, black pepper, garlic powder, and parsley. Drizzle over chickpeas and use your hands to coat chickpeas evenly in olive oil mixture. Spread evenly over pan.

4. Bake 20 minutes. Remove pan from oven and use a spatula to stir the chickpeas. Return pan to oven for another 15–20 minutes or until chickpeas are golden brown and crunchy. Remove from oven and cool completely before serving.

Nutrition

Calories: 366   **Fat:** 18g

Carbs: 32g   **Fiber:** 2.6g

Sugars: 9g   **Protein:** 17g

Add-On Options

- 2 (1-inch) slices French baguette: 140 calories
- Side salad, see page 30

Rollover Ingredient

low-fat cream cheese

CREAMY CAJUN PASTA

MAKES 8 SERVINGS

This creamy pasta is totally satisfying. It feels like a splurge, but at under 375 calories, it's a dinner that won't break the bank.

1 teaspoon extra-virgin olive oil

½ pound (8 ounces) smoked pork sausage, halved and cut into ¼-inch slices

1 small red onion, halved and sliced

3–4 cloves garlic, minced

2 red or yellow bell peppers, halved and sliced

1 (15-ounce) can diced tomatoes

1½ cups water (high elevations increase to 1¾ cup)

8 ounces pasta, like trottole

SAUCE

2 cups 1% milk

3 ounces low-fat cream cheese

1 teaspoon Cajun or Creole seasoning (like Tony Chachere's)

½ teaspoon smoked paprika

2 tablespoons all-purpose flour

2 tablespoons butter

1 teaspoon minced garlic

1 cup freshly grated Parmesan cheese

¼ cup fresh chopped parsley

1. Preheat olive oil in a large skillet over medium-high heat. Add sausage and cook 2–3 minutes, or until it starts to release oil and is browning. Add onion and cook until fragrant. Add garlic and sliced bell peppers. Cook until peppers are tender-crisp. Remove from heat and transfer sausage and peppers to a large plate. Set aside.

2. Return the pan to heat and add tomatoes and water. Bring to a boil over high heat, then quickly add pasta, reduce heat to medium-low, and cover. Cook until pasta is al dente and liquid is absorbed.

3. While the pasta is cooking, place milk, cream cheese, Cajun seasoning, paprika, and flour in a blender and blend until smooth.

4. Heat butter over medium heat in a medium saucepan. When melted, add garlic and cook 1–2 minutes or until tender and fragrant. Add mixture from the blender and cook until smooth and thickened; when the back of a spoon is dipped into the sauce, you should be able to trace your finger down the back and have the spot stay clean.

5. Remove sauce from heat and add Parmesan cheese. Stir until melted and smooth. Add parsley and stir to combine.

6. Add peppers and sausage to the pasta/tomato mixture and stir to combine. Add garlic sauce and combine. Season to taste with additional Cajun seasoning and serve immediately.

Nutrition

Calories: 253	Fat: 9g
Carbs: 36g	Fiber: 2g
Sugars: 4g	Protein: 8g

Add-On Options

- 16-ounces thinly sliced flank steak: 140 calories (per serving)
- 16-ounces thinly sliced chicken breast: 74 calories (per serving)
- 16-ounces peeled, deveined shrimp: 74 calories (per serving)
- 16-ounces firm tofu, drained and cut into 1-inch chunks: 50 calories (per serving)

    For the meat, season lightly with salt and pepper. Sauté with garlic and onions until done. Remove meat before adding eggs; return to pan with the noodles. If using tofu, add it when you add noodles into the sauce.

Cooking Tip

If you pre-chop the ingredients earlier in the day, or even the day before, this meal can come together in just a few minutes.

Shopping Tip

You can find many of the ingredients—specifically tamarind nectar (like Jumex)—in the Latin section of most grocery stores. Also, brown rice noodles are often found in the Asian food section of the grocery store.

Rollover Ingredients

cilantro, green onions, lime

PAD THAI

MAKES 6 SERVINGS

We cut down on the sugar and oil to lighten up this Asian favorite, but all the flavor is still there! Feel free to add shrimp, thinly sliced steak, or chicken breast to round out this tangy, slightly spicy meal.

SAUCE

¼ cup water

½ cup tamarind or mango nectar

3 tablespoons soy sauce or fish sauce

1 tablespoon extra-virgin olive oil

1 tablespoon freshly squeezed lime juice (about 1 small lime)

½–1 teaspoon Sriracha sauce

NOODLES

1 (12-ounce) package rice noodles

1½ teaspoons extra-virgin olive oil, divided

2 teaspoons minced garlic

¼ cup plus 2–3 tablespoons green onions, divided

3 eggs, whisked

2 teaspoons water

Pinch of kosher salt

1 (8-ounce) package fresh mung bean sprouts

¼ cup plus 2 tablespoons roasted salted peanuts, chopped and divided

¼ cup fresh cilantro, chopped

1½ limes, cut into 6 wedges

1. Bring 6 cups of water to a boil. While the water is heating, whisk together the sauce ingredients and set aside.

2. When the water begins to boil, place the rice noodles in a medium-sized, heat-safe bowl and pour water over noodles. Let them stand 6–8 minutes, stirring halfway through. Noodles should be not quite done; they'll finish cooking in the sauce.

3. While the noodles are cooking, heat 1 teaspoon olive oil in a large skillet over medium heat. Add garlic and green onions and cook for about 1 minute or until fragrant. Heat the remaining ½ teaspoon oil in the pan.

4. When hot, add eggs, water, and salt and cook for about 30 seconds, then, using a spatula, drag eggs across the pan to scramble them. Cook until just scrambled, then remove eggs and onions from the pan and set aside.

5. Add sauce ingredients to the pan and bring to a boil. When noodles are done softening, rinse immediately in cold water, then add to the boiling sauce.

6. Add mung bean sprouts and ¼ cup chopped peanuts. Cook until noodles are just barely tender. Return eggs to the pan and toss to combine. Sprinkle with chopped cilantro and chopped peanuts. Serve immediately with lime wedges.

Nutrition

Calories: 335   **Fat:** 11g

Carbs: 39g   **Fiber:** 4g

Sugars: 7g   **Protein:** 21g

Add-On Options

• Side salad, see page 30

• *Garlic Bread*

  1 slice whole wheat bread with 1½ teaspoons butter, 2 teaspoons crumbled Parmesan cheese, and garlic bread seasoning to taste. Broil until golden brown: 180 calories

Alternatives

Feel free to add your own favorite pizza toppings and vegetables, like olives, pepperoncinis, or spicy chili flakes. For a different spin on presentation, bake each serving in individual ramekins or oven-safe bowls.

PIZZA PASTA BAKE

MAKES 6 (1½-CUP) SERVINGS

"Pizza" in the title of any recipe is always a good thing. This dish takes all of the classic pizza pie flavors and packs them into one hearty, cheesy, family friendly casserole.

3 cups rotini pasta

1½ teaspoons extra-virgin olive oil

1 cup diced onion

1 medium green pepper, diced

1½ cups sliced mushrooms

4 cloves garlic, minced

8 ounces Italian turkey sausage links, casings removed

2 ounces turkey pepperoni, cut into quarters (about 1 cup)

1 (28-ounce) can diced tomatoes, drained

1 (15-ounce) can tomato sauce

½ tablespoon balsamic vinegar

½ tablespoon Italian seasoning

½ teaspoon marjoram

½ teaspoon kosher salt

1½ cups shredded mozzarella cheese

1. Preheat oven to 350 degrees F.

2. Cook pasta according to package directions; drain.

3. Heat an extra-large skillet to medium-high heat, add olive oil. Add onion and green pepper and stir frequently for about 5 minutes, until softened. Add mushrooms and garlic and cook for another 2 minutes, stirring often. Move vegetables to one side of pan and add sausage.

4. Use a spatula to break up meat into small pieces and continue cooking until cooked through. Add pepperoni and stir everything to combine.

5. Add diced tomatoes, tomato sauce, balsamic vinegar, Italian seasoning, marjoram, and salt. Bring tomato mixture to a low simmer and cook for 2–3 minutes. Turn off heat and add pasta, stirring to combine all ingredients.

6. Transfer mixture to a 9x13-inch baking dish and top with cheese. Bake for 30 minutes until cheese is melted and casserole is hot and bubbly throughout. Remove from oven and let rest for 5–10 minutes before serving.

Nutrition

Calories: 331   **Fat:** 12g

Carbs: 40g   **Fiber:** 3g

Sugars: 4g   **Protein:** 16g

Add-On Options

• 4 ounces grilled boneless, skinless chicken breast: 110 calories

• 4 ounces shrimp: 110 calories

Shopping Tip

Nutrition information was calculated for this recipe using traditional linguine; however, you're more than welcome to use whole wheat or Smart Pasta to reduce the carbs and increase the fiber.

Rollover Ingredient

low-fat cream cheese

Author's Note

I developed this recipe when I was expecting my third baby, Will, and I ate it at least once a week until he was born!—*Kate*

ROASTED ASPARAGUS AND MUSHROOM PASTA IN LEMON-CREAM SAUCE

MAKES 6 SERVINGS

This easy-yet-elegant, meatless creamy pasta dish has light, bright, springtime flavors and is perfect to serve to company. If you would like to add some additional protein, try some grilled chicken breast or shrimp.

1 pound asparagus, tough ends snapped off

4 cups whole mushrooms, thickly sliced

2–3 lemons

2 tablespoons extra-virgin olive oil

5–6 cloves garlic, minced or pressed

½ teaspoon kosher salt

¼ teaspoon freshly ground black pepper

¼ teaspoon Creole or coarse-grain mustard

8 ounces uncooked linguine

SAUCE

1½ cups 1% milk

¼ cup low-fat cream cheese

1½ tablespoons all-purpose flour

¾ teaspoon salt

1 tablespoon butter

2–3 garlic cloves, minced

¾ cups freshly grated Parmesan cheese

1. Preheat oven to 400 degrees F. Line a rimmed baking sheet with aluminum foil and set aside.

2. In a large bowl, combine trimmed asparagus and sliced mushrooms. Set aside. Zest lemons (enough to get 1 tablespoon of zest) and set the zest aside. Juice lemons and strain ¼ of the juice.

3. In a small bowl or measuring cup, combine the lemon juice, olive oil, garlic, salt, pepper, and mustard. Drizzle over vegetables and toss to combine. Spread vegetables onto the prepared baking sheet and roast in oven 20 minutes, or until asparagus is tender but not mushy. Remove from oven and allow to stand 5–10 minutes.

4. While vegetables are roasting, cook pasta al dente according to package directions.

5. To prepare sauce, combine milk, cream cheese, flour, and salt in a blender and blend until smooth.

6. In a large skillet, melt butter over medium heat and sauté the garlic for 1–2 minutes or until fragrant, being careful not to burn it. Add the milk mixture and stir until bubbling and thickened. Remove from heat and add the Parmesan cheese. Cover and allow to stand a few minutes, then remove lid and stir until smooth. Add the reserved lemon zest to the sauce.

7. When asparagus and mushrooms are done roasting, you can either portion out the pasta, vegetables, and sauce into individual servings or toss it all together.

Nutrition

(main dish serving)

Calories: 297	**Fat:** 7g
Carbs: 48g	**Fiber:** 3g
Sugars: 7g	**Protein:** 12g

Add-On Options

- 4 ounces grilled boneless skinless chicken breast: 110 calories
- 2 ounces crumbled Italian turkey sausage: 80 calories

Rollover Ingredients

basil, low-fat cream cheese

Author's Note

I use this zucchini ribbon method for other pasta dishes as well. I love the look of the thin green zucchini ribbons popping through. But if you'd like to be sneaky and get your kids to eat their vegetables, peel the zucchini first and they may not even notice it's in there!—*Sara*

ZUCCHINI RIBBONS AND PASTA WITH CREAMY LEMON-BASIL SAUCE

MAKES 4 MAIN DISH SERVINGS, OR 8 SMALL SIDES

This dish employs a brilliant tip for bulking up pasta dishes by adding vegetables. Tender zucchini are sliced in thin ribbons and cooked alongside the pasta, where they blend right in. A quick and easy cream sauce brings these bright Italian flavors together in a family-pleasing dish.

8 ounces fettuccine noodles	3–4 cloves finely minced garlic
1 medium zucchini	1 cup low-sodium chicken broth
2 teaspoons olive oil, divided	3½ ounces reduced-fat cream cheese
10 ounces grape tomatoes (about 2 cups)	½ cup freshly grated Parmesan cheese
Kosher salt	1 cup loosely packed fresh basil, chopped
Black pepper	1 tablespoon freshly squeezed lemon juice, more if desired

1. Cook pasta according to package instructions. While pasta is cooking, cut ends off zucchini and slice zucchini along the length into about ⅛-inch slices. Cut each of those slices into long ribbons, about the same size as the fettuccine. Set zucchini aside.

2. Heat a medium-sized skillet to medium heat. Add 1 teaspoon olive oil. Add tomatoes and a dash of kosher salt and black pepper. Cook, stirring frequently, for about 3–4 minutes, until tomatoes start to burst and look blistered. Remove tomatoes from pan and place in a small dish. Cover and set aside.

3. Add remaining olive oil to the empty pan and add garlic. Stir constantly on medium-low heat for about 30 seconds. Add chicken broth. Bring to a simmer and use a spatula to scrape any browned bits off the bottom of the pan. Simmer 1–2 minutes and then reduce heat to low.

4. Place cream cheese in a microwave-safe bowl and soften 20–30 seconds, until it can be easily stirred smooth. Ladle a couple spoonfuls of chicken broth mixture into the cream cheese and stir to combine. Once the mixture is smooth, add it to the pan with the remaining broth mixture and whisk until smooth and creamy.

5. Add Parmesan cheese, chopped basil, and lemon juice, and stir to combine. Season with salt and pepper to taste. (Lemon lovers can also squeeze in extra lemon juice at this point.)

6. When pasta is just about done, add zucchini strips to the pot and boil for about 2 minutes, or until zucchini is tender and pasta is done. Drain zucchini and pasta together and combine with sauce. Gently toss in tomatoes, or simply add them on top of each serving. Garnish with additional basil.

Nutrition

(¾ cup shredded chicken with sauce, plus 1 tablespoon shredded Parmesan)

Calories: 201 **Fat:** 14g

Carbs: 8g **Fiber:** 2g

Sugars: 5g **Protein:** 20g

Add-On Options

- ½ cup cooked pasta: 110 calories
- ½ cup white rice: 103 calories
- Small (2x2-inch) dinner roll: 80 calories
- 1 cup steamed broccoli with 1 teaspoon butter and ½ tablespoon Parmesan cheese: 91 calories

Cooking Tip

If you don't have a Dutch oven, you can cook the chicken and vegetables in a skillet on the stove top, then transfer everything to a 9x13-inch pan, cover tightly with foil, and then bake as directed.

Rollover Ingredient

basil

Author's Note

This dish is so easy to make, and the variations are endless. Eat it over pasta, rice, or couscous; pile it on a hoagie or dinner roll with fresh basil and a little extra cheese; or simply eat it straight from a bowl. —*Sara*

BRAISED ITALIAN CHICKEN

MAKES 6 (¾-CUP) SERVINGS

This rustic, hearty dish is deceptively simple to put together. The oven does the work here, melding comforting Italian flavors with tender bites of chicken that will please both kids and adults alike. This cold weather comfort food can be served a variety of ways.

1½–2 pounds boneless, skinless chicken thighs (6–8 thighs)

½ teaspoon kosher salt, divided

Freshly ground black pepper

2 teaspoons extra-virgin olive oil

1 cup diced onion

¼ cup shredded carrot

5–6 cloves garlic, minced

1 (14.5-ounce) can diced tomatoes, undrained

1 (14.5 ounce) can tomato sauce

2 teaspoons Italian seasoning

1 tablespoon balsamic vinegar, divided

2–3 tablespoons chopped fresh basil

Freshly shaved Parmesan cheese

1. Preheat oven to 350 degrees F.

2. To prepare chicken, rinse all pieces in cold water and use a pair of kitchen shears to snip off any excess fat. Blot dry on paper towels. Season one side of chicken with ¼ teaspoon kosher salt and several cracks of black pepper.

3. Heat a large Dutch oven to medium heat. When hot, add olive oil and brush across bottom of pot to cover surface. Add a quick spray of nonstick cooking spray if necessary. Place chicken in pan, seasoned-side down, and sprinkle remaining ¼ teaspoon salt plus a few cracks black pepper on other side of chicken. Cook 2–3 minutes. Flip chicken and cook for an additional 2–3 minutes. Remove chicken from pan and set aside.

4. Add onions and carrots to pot and cook 2–3 minutes, stirring often. Add garlic and cook for an additional 30 seconds, or until fragrant. Add can of diced tomatoes (including all the juices), tomato sauce, Italian seasoning, and ½ tablespoon balsamic vinegar. Stir ingredients, scraping up any browned bits on the bottom of the pot, and bring to a simmer.

5. Add chicken and all accumulated juices. Cover chicken with sauce and cover pot with lid or a double layer of aluminum foil.

6. Bake for 1 hour. Remove from oven and remove lid. Using 2 forks, gently shred chicken into large chunks. Add remaining ½ tablespoon balsamic vinegar and chopped basil. Add additional salt and pepper to taste.

7. Serve over pasta, rice, quinoa, or steamed vegetables, or on French rolls or slider buns. Garnish with fresh Parmesan cheese.

Nutrition

Calories: 321 **Fat:** 10g

Carbs: 17g **Fiber:** 1g

Sugar: 4g **Protein:** 37g

Add-On Options

- ½ cup cooked pasta: 110 calories
- 10 green beans (about 4 inches long), steamed: 17 calories

Alternatives

For an extra kid-friendly version, cut 1½ pounds boneless, skinless chicken breast into chunks and prepare in the same manner. Skip the cheese and serve with marinara, or low-fat ranch dip for dipping.

Author's Note

This is a great meal that's easily adapted for kids. I often make tenders for the adults at the table and cut a few tenders into nuggets for my little ones. Same prep—two meals. Everyone is happy!—*Sara*

CRISPY CHICKEN PARMESAN TENDERS

MAKES 6 SERVINGS; SERVING SIZE IS 2 CHICKEN STRIPS

These oven-baked tenders have a crispy coating that everyone loves. Serve them elegantly with a salad and vegetables, or dice into chunks for Italian chicken nuggets!

1½ pounds chicken tenders (12 tenders)

3 tablespoons all-purpose flour

1½ teaspoons seasoning salt

¼ teaspoon ground black pepper

2 egg whites

2½ cups corn flakes cereal

½ cup crumbled Parmesan cheese (from a jar/can)

2 teaspoons Italian seasoning

¾ cup shredded mozzarella cheese

1 cup plus 2 tablespoons jarred marinara sauce

1. Preheat oven to 450 degrees F. Line a baking sheet with foil and place a metal baking rack on top. Coat rack with nonstick cooking spray and set pan aside. Set out 3 shallow bowls for dredging.

2. Combine flour, seasoning salt, and black pepper in the first shallow bowl. Place egg whites in the second shallow bowl and whisk with a fork. Place corn flakes in a zip-top bag and use a rolling pin to crush them into fine crumbs. Add them to the third shallow bowl, along with Parmesan and Italian seasoning.

3. Working a couple of pieces at a time, place chicken tenders in flour mixture first, dipping to cover all sides and letting excess shake off. Then dip the chicken in the egg whites, and finally into the corn flake mixture, using your hands to press mixture into all sides.

4. Place chicken tenders on the baking rack and place pan in oven. Cook for 20 minutes, or until internal temperature of largest piece reaches 165 degrees F. Remove pan from oven and turn off oven. Sprinkle 1 tablespoon mozzarella cheese onto each tender. Return pan to oven (still turned off) until cheese melts, 1–2 minutes.

5. Divide chicken onto plates and top with 3 tablespoons marinara sauce or serve with marinara on the side for dipping.

Nutrition

Calories: 232	**Fat:** 9g
Carbs: 5.7g	**Fiber:** 2.1g
Sugars: 2.6g	**Protein:** 28.1g

Add-On Options

- ½ cup cooked pasta: 110 calories
- 4 ounces fresh asparagus (about 7–8 stalks), tossed with 1 tablespoon light balsamic vinaigrette and placed on the grill after you flip the chicken: 40 calories
- 2 (1-inch) slices French baguette: 140 calories
- Side salad, see page 30

Rollover Ingredient

fresh basil

GRILLED CHICKEN CAPRESE

MAKES 4 (4-OUNCE) SERVINGS

This chicken is quick and easy enough for weeknights, but it's so delicious and definitely fancy enough to serve to company. Be sure to get fresh mozzarella packed in water; it's usually available in the deli departments of grocery stores.

1 pound boneless, skinless chicken breasts

High-quality balsamic vinegar salad dressing

10 ounces grape tomatoes, halved

1 teaspoon minced garlic

½ cup fresh basil, torn

1 tablespoon extra-virgin olive oil

2 tablespoons balsamic vinegar

Salt and pepper to taste

4 (1-ounce) slices fresh mozzarella

1. Place chicken in a gallon-sized zip-top bag and add enough salad dressing to cover the chicken breasts (about 1 to 1½ cups). Marinate in the refrigerator at least 4 hours but no longer than 24 hours.

2. When ready to cook, preheat an outdoor grill. In a medium-sized bowl, gently combine halved tomatoes, garlic, and basil. Add olive oil and balsamic vinegar. Season to taste with salt and pepper and set aside.

3. Lightly oil the grates of the grill and reduce the cooking temperature to medium. (If you have a large grill, you can leave at least one cooking area on high.) Place chicken breasts on the grill, close the lid, and cook for 7 minutes. Flip the chicken and cook for another 7 minutes.

4. During the last 1–2 minutes, add a piece of fresh mozzarella to each chicken breast, close the lid, and allow cheese to melt. Remove from heat, top each chicken breast with the tomato-basil mixture, and serve immediately.

Nutrition

Calories: 197   **Fat:** 7g

Carbs: 6g   **Fiber:** 2g

Sugars: 4g   **Protein:** 26g

Add-On Options

- ½ cup cooked rice or quinoa with ½ tablespoon minced basil, ½ tablespoon crumbled reduced-fat feta, a squeeze of fresh lemon juice, and salt and pepper to taste: 116 calories
- 2 cups fresh spinach leaves sprinkled with ½ tablespoon low-fat feta, 1 teaspoon olive oil, 1 teaspoon balsamic vinegar, and salt and pepper to taste: 69 calories
- 2 tablespoons plain nonfat Greek yogurt mixed with ½ tablespoon reduced-fat feta and seasoned with salt and pepper (dollop on top of chicken and vegetables): 20 calories

Alternatives

Feel free to add or substitute any fresh grilling vegetables.

Cooking Tip

If using wooden skewers, place them in a pan and cover completely with water. Soak for a minimum of 30 minutes.

Rollover Ingredients

basil, oregano, rosemary

HERBED LEMON-GARLIC CHICKEN SKEWERS

MAKES 5 SERVINGS; SERVING SIZE IS 2 SKEWERS

Bright lemon and fresh herbs come together in a fast marinade that highlights summer vegetables and produces fast, flavorful results. Feel free to substitute any in-season grilling vegetable, or cook on an indoor grill during cooler months of the year.

10 (10-inch) wooden or metal skewers (see Cooking Tip)

MARINADE

1½ tablespoons finely minced or pressed garlic

1 tablespoon fresh lemon zest

4 tablespoons freshly squeezed lemon juice

½ cup minced fresh herbs, preferably a mix of basil, rosemary, and oregano

1 teaspoon kosher salt

¼ teaspoon ground black pepper

4 tablespoons extra-virgin olive oil

SKEWERS

2 medium zucchini, cut into ½-inch slices

1 large red bell pepper, cut into ¾-inch squares

1 medium red onion, cut into wedges and then ¾-inch squares

1¼ pounds boneless, skinless chicken breasts, cut into 1-inch cubes

Additional kosher salt and pepper

1 lemon cut into wedges, for serving

1. In a small bowl, combine garlic, lemon zest, lemon juice, herbs, salt, pepper, and olive oil. Set aside.

2. Place cut vegetables in a zip-top bag and add 3 tablespoons of the herb marinade. Toss to coat. Place chicken in a separate zip-top bag and add remaining marinade, tossing to coat. Let sit in the refrigerator for at least 30 minutes, and up to 4–6 hours.

3. Preheat grill to medium heat. Thread alternating meat and vegetables onto skewers. Lightly sprinkle with salt and pepper. Grill 3–4 minutes, and then flip. Continue cooking, flipping when necessary, until vegetables show grill marks and chicken is cooked through to 165 degrees F. Serve with lemon wedges to squeeze on top.

Nutrition

Calories: 342   Fat: 16g

Carbs: 9g   Fiber: 0g

Sugars: 8g   Protein: 38g

Add-On Options

• ½ cup cooked brown rice: 110 calories

• 1 cup steamed broccoli: 30 calories

Cooking Tip

If you'd like char marks on your drumsticks, place them on a foil-lined baking sheet under the broiler for just a minute while sauce is simmering during step 6.

Shopping Tip

Look for smaller drumsticks, 3–4 ounces each. A package of 2–2½ pounds should yield 10–12 drumsticks.

Author's Note

When a whole chicken is on the menu, my kids often fight over the drumsticks, so it's a special treat when I make an entire platter of drumsticks for dinner.—*Sara*

HONEY BALSAMIC DRUMSTICKS

MAKES 5–6 SERVINGS; SERVING SIZE IS 2 DRUMSTICKS

Chicken drumsticks are always popular, but a sweet and savory glaze makes these irresistible. Pair with a side of grains and your favorite vegetable, and an easy dinner is on the table in no time.

2–2½ pounds chicken drumsticks (10–12 drumsticks)

½ teaspoon kosher salt

¼ teaspoon ground black pepper

½ teaspoon paprika

¾ teaspoon onion powder

3 teaspoons olive oil, divided

SAUCE

2 tablespoons honey

2 tablespoons balsamic vinegar

2 tablespoons ketchup

4 cloves garlic, minced or pressed

2 tablespoons water

1. Preheat oven to 350 degrees F.

2. Rinse chicken, pat dry, and set aside. In a small bowl, combine salt, pepper, paprika, and onion powder. Drizzle chicken with 1 teaspoon olive oil and use clean hands to coat all pieces. Sprinkle spice mixture over chicken and massage in.

3. Heat large Dutch oven (or heavy oven-proof skillet with an oven-proof lid) to medium heat. Add 2 teaspoons olive oil and brush to cover bottom of entire pan. If more is needed, add a light spray of nonstick cooking spray. Brown chicken 2 minutes per side. (Cook in batches if necessary.)

4. While chicken is searing, whisk sauce ingredients together in a small bowl. Add to pan after chicken has been seared. Gently toss chicken to coat. Cover pan and transfer to oven.

5. Bake for 20 minutes, rotate chicken pieces, and baste with sauce. Bake an additional 20 minutes. Remove chicken from oven and place drumsticks on a plate, covered with foil to keep warm.

6. Bring sauce that remains in the pan to a boil on stove top and simmer, uncovered, for 4–5 minutes until thick and glazy. Return chicken to pan and gently toss in glaze. If desired, place chicken on a platter and cover with sauce. Let sit for 5 minutes before serving.

Nutrition

(white meat, no skin)

Calories: 191	Fat: 6g
Carbs: 1g	Fiber: 0g
Sugars: 0g	Protein: 33g

(dark meat, no skin)

Calories: 265	Fat: 15g
Carbs: 1g	Fiber: 0g
Sugars: 0g	Protein: 30g

(roasted sweet potatoes)

Calories: 170	Fat: 7g
Carbs: 25g	Fiber: 4g
Sugars: 7g	Protein: 2g

Serving Suggestion

For a delicious salad, toss together 3 ounces leftover breast meat, 5 cups leafy greens, ½ cup black beans, ½ cup cherry tomatoes, and 5 red onion slices: 245 calories, plus your favorite dressing

Rollover Ingredients

chipotle chilies, cilantro, lime

ROASTED GARLIC-LIME CHIPOTLE CHICKEN

MAKES 6 (4-OUNCE) SERVINGS

Roasting a whole chicken in a slow cooker guarantees tender, juicy, fall-off-the-bones meat, and the herbs, spices, and limes in this recipe ensure this chicken is full of flavor. For a delicious dinner, serve with Smoky Roasted Sweet Potatoes.

1 (4-pound) whole chicken

2 tablespoons butter, sfotened

2 cloves garlic, minced

2 tablespoons finely minced cilantro

1 tablespoon adobo sauce from canned chipotle chilies

½ heaping teaspoon kosher salt

Zest of 1 lime

SPICE RUB

½ teaspoon garlic powder

½ teaspoon onion powder

¼ teaspoon ground coriander

½ teaspoon coarsely ground salt

½ teaspoon freshly ground black pepper

1–2 teaspoons dark brown sugar

Enough freshly squeezed lime juice to make a slightly runny paste (about 1 tablespoon)

STUFFING

4–5 cloves garlic

½ cup cilantro

1 onion, halved

1. Loosen chicken skin by sliding your hand between the skin and the breast and wiggling it around. In a small bowl, combine butter, garlic, cilantro, adobo, salt, and lime zest. Rub mixture under the skin of the chicken.

2. In a separate small bowl, combine all ingredients for the chicken rub. Massage rub all over the chicken. Stuff inside of chicken with whole cloves of garlic, the spent limes, cilantro, and onion. If desired, sprinkle the whole chicken with very coarse salt and black pepper. Tie legs together with twine to help chicken keep its shape while cooking.

3. Place 3 fist-sized pieces of balled-up aluminum foil in the bottom of a slow cooker and place the chicken on it, breast side up. Cook on low 6–8 hours.

SMOKY ROASTED SWEET POTATOES

MAKES 6 (½-CUP) SERVINGS

¼ cup extra-virgin olive oil

1 teaspoon kosher salt

1 teaspoon freshly ground black pepper

1½ teaspoons smoked paprika

1½ teaspoons minced garlic

1 tablespoon cornstarch

1½ pounds peeled sweet potatoes, cut into ¼-inch cubes

1. Preheat oven to 425 degrees F. Line a baking sheet with aluminum foil and spray with nonstick cooking spray.

2. In a large bowl, whisk together olive oil, salt, pepper, paprika, garlic, and cornstarch. Toss sweet potatoes in the seasoning mixture and spread evenly over the prepared baking sheet.

3. Bake in preheated oven 30–35 minutes or until the outsides are crispy and the insides are tender, flipping the potatoes once halfway through.

Nutrition

Calories: 140   **Fat:** 5g

Carbs: 4g   **Fiber:** 0g

Sugars: 1g   **Protein:** 21g

Cooking Tip

When serving this taco chicken, you can offer a variety of toppings that will add a lot of deliciousness without adding a lot of calories. If you're watching your carbs, this chicken is delicious served on a plate with some (or all!) of these toppings and eaten with a fork.

Alternatives

Instead of using a tortilla, make a salad using this chicken and your favorite toppings.

Rollover Ingredient

lime

SLOW COOKER TACO CHICKEN

MAKES 10 (3-OUNCE) SERVINGS

This easy slow cooker recipe is perfect for busy nights or for entertaining. Let the chicken simmer all day, and then you just need to set out favorite taco toppings like avocado, Pico de Gallo, and crumbled cheese.

2 pounds boneless, skinless chicken breasts

½ cup Italian salad dressing (not low-fat)

1 (1-ounce) packet Ranch dressing seasoning

½ cup water

1½ teaspoons chili powder

1½ teaspoons ground cumin

1 teaspoon coriander

6–8 cloves garlic, smashed

1 tablespoon dehydrated onion

Juice of 1 lime

Salt, to taste

Chipotle hot sauce, to taste

Place all ingredients except for lime, salt, and hot sauce in slow cooker and cook 5–6 hours on low, or until chicken shreds easily with a fork. When done, shred the chicken and sprinkle with lime juice. Taste and season with salt and chipotle hot sauce to taste.

Freezer Instructions: Combine all ingredients except lime, salt, and hot sauce in a large zip-top bag and freeze. When ready to cook, place the frozen mixture in slow cooker for 6–8 hours on low. Before serving, add lime juice, salt, and hot sauce.

TACO BAR

Add-On Options	Calories	Fat	Carbs	Fiber	Sugar	Protein
Lime wedge	Free!					
2 tablespoons chopped cilantro	Free!					
4 onion slices	10	0g	1g	0g	0g	1g
2 tablespoons Pico de Gallo	10	0g	1g	1g	0g	1g
2 tablespoons green salsa	15	0.5g	2g	1g	1g	0g
1 tablespoon light sour cream	20	1g	1g	0g	1g	1g
1 tablespoon cotija or queso fresco	20	2g	0g	0g	0g	1g
⅛ avocado	31	3g	2g	1g	0g	0g
6-inch whole wheat tortilla	90	2g	15g	2g	0g	3g

Nutrition

Calories: 261	Fat: 5g
Carbs: 18g	Fiber: 4g
Sugars: 8g	Protein: 38g

Add-On Options

- 1 cup sliced fresh mango: 107 calories
- ½ cup cooked brown rice: 110 calories

Cooking Tip

These servings are very large. If you have little eaters (or little appetites), this recipe will easily serve 6.

Shopping Tip

You can use seedless baby cucumbers in this recipe and not have to seed them.

Rollover Ingredients

ginger, green onions, cilantro, lime

Author's Note

This is one of my favorite meals when I feel like I need to lighten things up, like after the holidays or a vacation when I haven't been eating as well as I should have.—*Kate*

SPICY TURKEY LETTUCE WRAPS

MAKES 4 SERVINGS

These lettuce wraps are packed with vegetables, protein, and flavor. It's easy to adjust the heat level before you add the crisp carrots, peppers, and cucumbers and round it all out with crunchy cashews.

20 ounces extra-lean (99% lean) ground turkey

¼ cup chopped green onion

6 cloves garlic, minced

1 tablespoon minced fresh ginger

1 tablespoon extra-virgin olive oil

4 tablespoons freshly squeezed lime juice

1 tablespoon soy sauce

1 tablespoon brown sugar

Sriracha sauce, to taste (start with ½ teaspoon and adjust from there)

1½ cups seeded and diced cucumber

1 medium red bell pepper, seeded and chopped

½ cup shredded carrot

¼ cup chopped cilantro

¼ cup chopped cashews

16 lettuce leaves (Boston Bibb, butter lettuce, or trimmed iceberg lettuce)

1. In a medium bowl, combine ground turkey, green onion, garlic, and ginger. Set aside.

2. Heat 1 tablespoon olive oil in a large skillet over medium-high heat. Cook turkey mixture until it's brown and crumbly.

3. While the turkey is cooking, combine the lime juice, soy sauce, brown sugar, and Sriracha sauce. Set aside.

4. Place the diced cucumber, bell pepper, carrot, cilantro, and cashews in a large bowl. When the turkey is done cooking, add it to the vegetable mixture. Drizzle with the sauce and toss to combine. Serve immediately in leaves of lettuce.

Nutrition

Calories: 305　　**Fat:** 13g

Carbs: 28g　　**Fiber:** 16g

Sugars: 2g　　**Protein:** 27g

Add-On Options

- 2 tablespoons light sour cream: 40 calories
- 2 (¼-inch) slices avocado: 50 calories
- Side salad, see page 30
- Fresh squeeze of lime juice: 0 calories

Author's Note

I've been making this recipe since my husband and I got married in 2001, and even after all these years and all these recipes, *this* is his number-one favorite meal that I make.—*Kate*

BURRITO PIE

MAKES 12 SERVINGS

Casseroles don't have to be heavy and fat-laden, even when cheese is involved. This "Mexican lasagna" is full of flavor and uses a lot of ingredients you probably already have in your pantry and refrigerator.

½ pound 93% lean ground beef

1 medium onion, chopped

3–4 cloves garlic, minced

1 packet taco seasoning

1 (2-ounce) can sliced black olives, drained (or a handful of medium black olives, chopped)

1 (4-ounce) can roasted green chilies, undrained

1 (15.5-ounce) can diced tomatoes with green chilies

1½ cups corn (either frozen or a 15.5-ounce can of corn, drained)

1 cup enchilada sauce

1 (15.5-ounce) can refried or black beans (if using black beans, drain and rinse them first)

6 large (burrito-size) whole wheat tortillas, 3 of them cut in half

3 cups shredded cheddar, Colby Jack, or Pepper Jack cheese (or a combination)

1. Preheat oven to 350 degrees F.

2. Brown the ground beef in a large skillet over medium heat. When the beef is about halfway cooked, add onion and garlic. Cook until the beef is done and onions and garlic are tender and fragrant.

3. Add taco seasoning and stir to combine. Add the black olives, chilies, tomatoes, corn, enchilada sauce, and refried beans. Bring to a simmer then remove from heat.

4. Spread about ½ cup of the mixture onto the bottom of a 9×13-inch pan. Top with one whole tortilla and one half tortilla. Spread 1½ cups of the mixture on top of the tortillas, sprinkle with cheese, then top with another one and a half tortillas. Repeat layers of meat, tortillas, and cheese until all tortillas are used.

5. Bake 25–30 minutes or until heated through and the cheese is melted and bubbly.

Nutrition

Calories: 380 Fat: 16g

Carbs: 27g Fiber: 4g

Sugars: 5g Protein: 31g

Add-On Options

- 2 (¼-inch) slices avocado: 50 calories
- 1 tablespoon bottled barbecue sauce: (check calories on bottle)
- ½ cup grapes: 52 calories
- 1 ounce Kettle-style potato chips (about 13 chips): 150 calories

Alternatives

Going low-carb? Ditch the bun and wrap everything in lettuce leaves instead.

Shopping Tip

Look for medium-sized buns around 110–120 calories each. We also love these burgers on soft, sweet Hawaiian-style buns.

Author's Note

If you dislike mushrooms, don't be dismayed! Mincing the mushrooms not only bulks up the burgers, but keeps them juicy and moist. No one will even know they are in there since finely minced mushrooms blend right into the ground beef.—*Sara*

CHEDDAR BACON BURGERS WITH CARAMELIZED ONIONS

MAKES 5 SERVINGS

Sometimes eating healthy makes you feel like you have to give up everything you love. Cure that mentality with this juicy, flavorful burger. Real beef, cheese, and even bacon make appearances here, reminding you that calorie-counting can still taste amazing.

1 pound 96% lean ground beef

8 ounces small brown mushrooms, such as cremini or baby bella

3 teaspoons extra-virgin olive oil, divided

1 tablespoon Worcestershire sauce

½ tablespoon Creole mustard (or any coarse grain or Dijon mustard)

1 teaspoon minced garlic

½ teaspoon smoked paprika

1 teaspoon kosher salt

½ teaspoon freshly ground black pepper

2 cups thinly sliced onion

½ cup plus 2 tablespoons shredded sharp cheddar cheese

3 tablespoons plus 1 teaspoon light mayonnaise

5 lettuce leaves

10 slices ripe tomato

5 slices precooked thin cut bacon, heated according to package instructions

5 whole-grain rolls or buns, 3–4 inches in diameter

1. Place beef in a mixing bowl and break up with a fork very gently. Set aside.

2. Remove stems from mushrooms and finely mince. You may use a food processor for this step if you choose, pulsing several times until mushrooms are finely chopped. Heat a medium-sized skillet to medium heat. Add 1½ teaspoons olive oil and minced mushrooms. Stir occasionally until mushrooms are golden brown and fragrant, about 4–5 minutes. Remove from heat and set aside.

3. To make burgers, add Worcestershire, mustard, garlic, smoked paprika, salt, and pepper to beef. Add in cooked mushrooms. Use a fork to very gently combine ingredients, but don't overmix.

4. Preheat grill to medium-high heat. Return pan used for mushrooms to medium heat and add remaining 1½ teaspoons olive oil. Add onions and stir often until soft and golden, about 15 minutes. Season with a pinch of kosher salt.

5. While onions are cooking, form beef mixture into 5 equal patties, about 4 inches in diameter. Grill 3–5 minutes, then flip once and continue cooking until internal temperature reaches 160 degrees F. Turn off heat and sprinkle about 2 tablespoons of cheese onto each patty.

6. If desired, toast buns on hot grill or hot pan. Spread 1 teaspoon of light mayo on each half. Place lettuce leaves on bottom bun, top with 2 tomato slices, burger, and one slice bacon, cut in half. Divide onions evenly among burgers and top with top half of bun.

Nutrition

(meat loaf only)

Calories: 187   **Fat:** 5g

Carbs: 21g   **Fiber:** 0g

Sugars: 16g   **Protein:** 13g

(⅓ cup sweet potatoes)

Calories: 86   **Fat:** 0g

Carbs: 20g   **Fiber:** 3g

Sugars: 7g   **Protein:** 2g

Add-On Options

• 10 green beans (about 4-inches long), steamed and tossed with ¼ teaspoon olive oil, salt, and pepper: 57 calories

Cooking Tip

This recipe is designed so the sweet potatoes and meat loaf can cook together. However, cooking time varies for sweet potatoes, depending on size, so place them in the oven as soon as it's preheated. That way if the potatoes need longer than the meat loaf, everything can still be done at the same time.

Shopping Tip

Find small cans of chipotle peppers in adobo sauce in the Latin foods aisle. These peppers are spicy so one small minced pepper will give the entire loaf mild heat and flavor. If you enjoy heat, add 2 peppers. For the glaze, use the sauce from the can (which is not spicy, just flavorful) without peppers.

CHIPOTLE GLAZED MEAT LOAF WITH SPICED SWEET POTATOES

MAKES 8 SERVINGS; SERVING SIZE IS 2 (½-INCH) SLICES MEAT LOAF WITH ⅓ CUP SWEET POTATOES

If you think meat loaf is old-school, think again. Our version gives a whole new spin to Grandma's classic dish. Mild heat and smokiness pair perfectly with mashed sweet potatoes. Slip leftovers in a whole-grain hoagie or wrap for a killer meat loaf sandwich.

SWEET POTATOES

4 (8-ounce) sweet potatoes (about 2 pounds)

1 teaspoon honey

¼ teaspoon ground cumin

¼ teaspoon kosher salt

⅛ teaspoon black pepper

GLAZE

¾ cup ketchup

6 tablespoons brown sugar

1½ tablespoons cider vinegar

1½ tablespoons adobo sauce from canned chipotle peppers

MEAT LOAF

2 teaspoons vegetable oil

1 cup finely diced onion

3 cloves garlic, minced

1 large jalapeño

½ pound lean ground beef

½ pound ground pork

⅔ cup panko bread crumbs

⅓ cup chopped cilantro

1–2 chipotle peppers in adobo sauce, seeds removed, and peppers minced

2 eggs

½ teaspoon chili powder

½ teaspoon dry oregano

¼ teaspoon kosher salt

½ teaspoon black pepper

2 teaspoons Dijon mustard

2 teaspoons Worcestershire sauce

1 teaspoon liquid smoke

½ cup buttermilk

2 teaspoons adobo sauce from a can of chipotle peppers

1. Preheat oven to 350 degrees F.

2. Wash and dry sweet potatoes and prick with a fork. Wrap sweet potatoes in foil. Place in oven and bake for 1 hour, or until potatoes are easily pierced with a knife. (See Cooking Tip on page 84.)

3. Prepare glaze by mixing ketchup, brown sugar, cider vinegar, and adobo sauce in a small saucepan and bring to a simmer. Simmer 3–5 minutes until slightly thickened. Set aside.

4. To prepare meat loaf, heat oil in medium skillet. Add onion, garlic, and jalapeño and sauté until softened, about 5 minutes. Set aside to cool.

5. Place beef and pork in a mixing bowl. Add panko, cilantro, and minced chipotle pepper. Set aside.

6. In a separate bowl, mix eggs with chili powder, oregano, salt, pepper, Dijon mustard, Worcestershire, liquid smoke, buttermilk, and 2 teaspoons adobo sauce. Whisk to combine.

7. Add onion mixture to meat and use a fork or clean hands to gently combine. Add egg mixture and continue to mix.

8. With wet hands, form mixture into a free form loaf about 9x5 inches. Place on a foil-lined shallow baking pan. Divide glaze and set aside half for later. Glaze meat loaf with remaining glaze and place in oven for approximately 60 minutes, or until internal temperature reaches 160 degrees F. Let rest 5 minutes before slicing.

9. While meat loaf is resting, mash sweet potatoes. Slice in half, scoop insides into a mixing bowl, and add honey, cumin, salt, and pepper. Mash well.

10. Serve meat loaf with reserved glaze, reheated until warm.

Nutrition

(using ground turkey)

Calories: 319   **Fat:** 9g

Carbs: 36g   **Fiber:** 3g

Sugars: 14g   **Protein:** 23g

Add-On Options

- 1 (¾-inch) slice fresh pineapple: 42 calories
- Side salad, see page 30
- 3 ounces frozen sweet potato fries: 140 calories
- 1 ounce vegetable chips (like Terra): 150 calories
- 1 cup cubed watermelon: 46 calories

Shopping Tip

Not all ground turkey is created equal; some varieties can have as much (or more!) fat and calories as ground beef. Be sure to check the nutritional information on the packaging so you don't unknowingly sabotage your healthy eating plans.

Rollover Ingredient

fresh ginger

HAWAIIAN SLOPPY JOES

MAKES 8 SERVINGS

Sautéing onions, garlic, and chopped bell peppers in bacon drippings adds lots of flavor, and using just a few slices of center-cut bacon helps keep the calorie count under control. Serve on whole wheat buns with your favorite fresh, crunchy vegetables.

6 ounces center-cut bacon

20 ounces extra-lean (93% lean) ground turkey or beef

1 medium onion, diced

1 green pepper, diced

3–4 cloves garlic, minced

1 teaspoon fresh minced ginger

¾ cup ketchup

2 tablespoons brown sugar

1 tablespoon cider vinegar

½ teaspoon hickory-flavored liquid smoke

1 tablespoon soy sauce

⅓–½ cup pineapple juice

Salt and freshly ground black pepper, to taste

8 whole wheat buns or rolls

Pineapple rings, red onion slices, and/or banana peppers (optional)

1. Preheat oven to 425 degrees F. Lay each slice of bacon flat on a foil-lined baking sheet and bake for 15–18 minutes or until bacon is crisp. Remove from oven and drain bacon on a paper towel-lined plate, reserving 2 tablespoons of the bacon drippings.

2. Place bacon drippings in a large skillet and heat to medium heat. Add the ground turkey or beef, onion, and pepper and cook until the meat is about halfway cooked. Add the garlic and ginger and cook until the meat is completely cooked (about 6–7 minutes.)

3. While the meat is cooking, whisk the ketchup, brown sugar, vinegar, liquid smoke, and soy sauce together in a small bowl. Add the sauce to meat. Add pineapple juice, keeping in mind that the sauce will thicken. Bring to a simmer, then cover and reduce heat to low. Cook 20–25 minutes, stirring occasionally, until peppers and onions are tender.

4. Crumble the cooked bacon and add it to the meat mixture. Season to taste with salt and black pepper. Serve on whole wheat hamburger buns with a slice of pineapple, a slice of red onion, and, if desired, a few banana pepper rings.

Slow Cooker Instructions: Brown meat with onion, green pepper, garlic, and ginger. Transfer to a slow cooker. Add sauce and combine well. Cook on low for 3–4 hours. Before serving, add the cooked and crumbled bacon and season to taste with salt and pepper. Serve as directed.

Freezer Instructions: Brown meat with onion, green pepper, garlic, and ginger. Transfer to a heavy-duty zip-top bag or freezer container. Add sauce and cooked, crumbled bacon and freeze. To cook, place frozen mixture in a slow cooker and cook on low 3–5 hours. Serve as directed.

Nutrition

Calories: 294   Fat: 16g

Carbs: 8g   Fiber: 3g

Sugars: 3g   Protein: 30g

Add-On Options

• ½ cup cooked quinoa or brown rice with a squeeze of lime juice, ½ teaspoon olive oil, and salt and pepper to taste: 130 calories

• ½ cup canned black beans, rinsed and drained, and heated with desired seasonings (we suggest a dash of cumin, garlic, salt, and pepper): 120 calories

• 1 small tortilla: 110 calories (flour), 50 calories (corn)

Cooking Tip

No outdoor grill? Cook on an indoor grill pan, and cook tomatoes in a nonstick skillet on the stove top.

Shopping Tip

Can't find skirt steak? Try flank steak instead.

Rollover Ingredients

cilantro, lime

Author's Note

I will take Pico de Gallo in any form, which was the inspiration for this meal. It's one of my absolute favorites, especially when eaten on the back porch on a warm summer night.—Sara

GRILLED PICO STEAK

MAKES 6 SERVINGS; SERVING SIZE IS 4-OUNCES STEAK WITH ⅔-CUP VEGETABLE MIXTURE

A quick and easy marinade makes this steak perfect for a weeknight dinner or for entertaining guests.

1¾ pounds skirt steak

1 lime

2 cloves garlic, minced

1½ teaspoons liquid smoke

2 tablespoons white vinegar

2 teaspoons extra-virgin olive oil

½ teaspoon chili powder

1 teaspoon kosher salt

½ teaspoon freshly ground black pepper

2 cups grape or cherry tomatoes

1 small to medium red onion

1 medium ripe avocado

¼ cup chopped cilantro

1. Place steak in a shallow baking pan. Zest lime and place zest in a small bowl. Reserve remaining lime. To the bowl of lime zest, add garlic, liquid smoke, vinegar, olive oil, chili powder, salt, and pepper. Stir to combine and then rub over both sides of steak. Let steak rest at room temperature for at least 30 minutes, or up to 4 hours in the fridge.

2. Preheat barbecue grill to medium high heat. Layer 2 sheets of heavy-duty foil, about 10x10-inches. Fold up edges of foil to create a small "pan." Place tomatoes on the foil pan and spray lightly with cooking spray.

3. Cut the top off onion and remove outer papery layer, leaving root intact. Cut onion into 8 wedges through the root, so that each wedge is being held together with a small piece of the root. Spray each wedge lightly with cooking spray and add to foil pan with tomatoes.

4. Place steak on hot grill. Place both foil pan of tomatoes and onion directly on grill surface. (If you have an upper rack on your grill, place vegetables there.) Cook steak for about 5 minutes on each side, or until an internal thermometer registers 135 degrees F. Remove steak from grill and tent with foil for at least 5 minutes before slicing.

5. Lightly toss tomatoes until charred and skins just barely start to split. Turn onion until slightly softened and grill marks appear. Remove vegetables from heat as soon as they are finished cooking.

6. While steak is resting, chop onion wedges into large chunks, discarding root tips. Place tomatoes and onion in a bowl. Add the juice from reserved lime and cilantro. Cut avocado into chunks, and add. Salt and pepper to taste. Gently toss together.

7. Slice steak into thin strips and top each serving with tomato mixture.

Nutrition

Calories: 329   **Fat:** 18g

Carbs: 14g   **Fiber:** 3g

Sugars: 4g   **Protein:** 27g

Add-On Options

• 1 cup cubed watermelon: 46 calories

Cooking Tip

If you can't find Greek herb seasoning, combine ½ teaspoon dried oregano, ¼ teaspoon dried basil, ¼ teaspoon dried mint, and a pinch of kosher salt.

Shopping Tip

When shopping for Greek seasoning, avoid ground Greek seasoning; you'll want one that has the dehydrated herb leaves. (Our favorite is McCormick Greek Seasoning.)

Rollover Ingredient

plain Greek yogurt

GRILLED STEAK GYRO PITAS

MAKES 6 SERVINGS

This has become one of Kate's family's favorite meals. The marinade is just a few pantry ingredients and makes the steak unbelievably tender and flavorful.

MARINADE

1½ pounds flank steak

½ cup extra-virgin olive oil

½ cup red wine vinegar

¾ teaspoon kosher salt

1 teaspoon Greek herb seasoning

1 teaspoon sugar

1 teaspoon minced garlic

PITAS

½ cup plain fat-free Greek yogurt

3–4 green onions, chopped

1 large clove garlic, minced

1 teaspoon red wine vinegar

Salt and pepper, to taste

6 whole wheat pita halves

1 cup grape tomatoes

1 medium cucumber, peeled, halved, seeded, and sliced

1 small red onion, thinly sliced

1 cup red leaf lettuce or baby spinach leaves, optional

1. Lightly score flank steak in a crisscrossing diagonal pattern and place in a gallon zip-top bag. In a small bowl, whisk together the olive oil, red wine vinegar, salt, Greek seasoning, sugar, and garlic and pour over the steak. Marinate at least 4 hours, up to 24 hours.

2. When ready to serve, whisk together Greek yogurt, green onions, garlic, and red wine vinegar. Season with salt and pepper to taste and set aside.

3. Preheat grill to high. Lightly oil grill grates and place steak on grill. Decrease heat to medium-high. Sear 5–8 minutes per side or until internal temperature reaches 135 degrees F. Remove from heat, place steak on a cutting board, and use a piece of aluminum foil to form a tent over the steak. Allow steak to rest 5 minutes before cutting it into thin slices against the grain.

4. Divide steak evenly among the 6 pita halves. Top with grape tomatoes, cucumber slices, and red onion slices. Top with yogurt sauce and serve immediately.

Nutrition

Calories: 340   **Fat:** 12g

Carbs: 20g   **Fiber:** 3g

Sugars: 4g   **Protein:** 36g

Alternatives

You may substitute white rice, wild rice, or quinoa.

Shopping Tip

Look for small bags of precooked rice at the grocery store. They steam up quickly in the microwave, saving you prep time in the kitchen. Since you only need a small amount, you could also cook extra rice another night of the week and save a little for this recipe.

Rollover Ingredient

feta cheese

MEDITERRANEAN STEAK AND RICE BOWLS

MAKES 6 SERVINGS; SERVING SIZE IS 4-OUNCES STEAK WITH 1 CUP RICE MIXTURE

Bursting with healthy vegetables, whole-grain rice, and protein-packed flank steak, this satisfying, well-rounded meal brings the flavors of the Mediterranean right into your kitchen. Eat it for dinner or keep it in the fridge for a quick reheated lunch.

MARINADE

Zest from 1 lemon

¼ cup freshly squeezed lemon juice

¼ cup white vinegar

4 cloves garlic, roughly chopped

1½ teaspoon sugar

1 teaspoon seasoned salt

¼ teaspoon pepper

¼ teaspoon red pepper flakes

1 teaspoon Italian seasoning

¼ teaspoon oregano

4 tablespoons water

4 tablespoons extra-virgin olive oil

STEAK AND RICE

2 pounds flank steak

Kosher salt

Freshly ground black pepper

½ teaspoon extra-virgin olive oil

1 medium zucchini, sliced in half lengthwise, and then in ¼-inch slices

2 cups grape tomatoes

1 (6-ounce) jar marinated artichoke hearts, drained and roughly chopped

2 cups cooked brown rice

¼ cup chopped fresh parsley

6 tablespoons reduced-fat feta cheese

1. Place all marinade ingredients, except oil, in a blender. Blend for a few seconds, and then, with blender on low, slowly drizzle in olive oil. Set aside ¼ cup of marinade and store in refrigerator. Place remaining marinade in shallow pan or large zip-top bag. Add flank steak and refrigerate at least 4–6 hours, rotating occasionally to evenly distribute marinade.

2. When ready to cook, remove steak and sprinkle lightly on both sides with kosher salt and freshly ground black pepper. You may cook steak in one of 3 ways:

    Broil: Preheat broiler and place steak on a broiler pan. Cook for about 5–8 minutes on each side, or until top is browned and internal temperature reaches 135 degrees F.

Outdoor grill: Heat grill to high heat. Lightly oil grill grates and place steak on grill. Decrease heat to medium-high. Sear 5–8 minutes per side or until internal temperature reaches 135 degrees F.

Indoor grill pan: Heat indoor grill pan to medium-high heat. Once pan is hot (water droplets should sizzle when dropped on pan) brush pan lightly with vegetable oil. Place steak on pan and cook 5–8 minutes. Flip steak and cook another 5-8 minutes until internal temperature reaches 135 degrees F.

3. While steak is cooking, heat a large sauté pan to medium heat. When hot, add ½ teaspoon olive oil and zucchini. Season with a pinch of kosher salt and 2–3 cracks black pepper. Cook 2–3 minutes, stirring often, until softened.

4. Add tomatoes, and continue to cook and stir occasionally, until tomato skins are slightly blistered and tomatoes start to burst. Add artichokes and stir to heat. Add rice and continue to stir until heated through. Remove from heat and stir in parsley, feta, and reserved ¼ cup marinade.

5. When steak is done cooking, place on cutting board and tent with foil. Let rest 5 minutes before slicing steak thinly across the grain. Serve over rice mixture.

Nutrition

(pot roast)

Calories: 239	**Fat:** 10g
Carbs: 5g	**Fiber:** 1g
Sugars: 2g	**Protein:** 30g

(roasted vegetables)

Calories: 135	**Fat:** 7g
Carbs: 16g	**Fiber:** 1g
Sugars: 2g	**Protein:** 2g

Add-On Options

• *Creamy Horseradish Sauce*

Whisk together 1 cup plain fat-free Greek yogurt, 2 teaspoons minced garlic, 2 teaspoons prepared horseradish, and 1 bunch of chopped green onions (about ¼ cup). Season with kosher salt and freshly ground black pepper, to taste: 17 calories per 1½ tablespoons

Shopping Tip

Finding the right cut of meat for a pot roast can be surprisingly tricky. The best choices for leaner pot roasts are either bottom round roasts or top round roasts.

Rollover Ingredient

plain Greek yogurt

SLOW COOKER POT ROAST

MAKES 12 SERVINGS

Everyone needs an easy, melt-in-your-mouth pot roast in their arsenal of recipes! At our house, we'll serve this with Italian Roasted Vegetables the first day, then use the leftover roast for sandwiches, tacos, or salads another day.

1 tablespoon steak seasoning (like McCormick Grill Mates Montreal Steak Seasoning)

3½ pounds bottom round roast

3 tablespoons extra-virgin olive oil

1 (1-ounce) packet onion soup mix

1 large sweet onion, sliced

10 cloves garlic, smashed

2 cups vegetable broth

¼ cup red wine vinegar

1. Sprinkle steak seasoning over roast and use your hands to rub it into the meat. In a large skillet, heat olive oil over high heat. When very hot, carefully add the roast and sear 2–3 minutes on each side, until browned. Place the seared roast in a slow cooker.

2. Sprinkle onion soup mix over roast and cover with sliced onion and garlic. Add vegetable broth and red wine vinegar.

3. Cook roast on high 4–6 hours or on low 6–8 hours or until the roast shreds easily with a fork.

ITALIAN ROASTED VEGETABLES

MAKES 8 SERVINGS

¼ cup extra-virgin olive oil

1 teaspoon kosher salt

½ teaspoon freshly ground black pepper

1 tablespoon Italian seasoning (or 2 tablespoons chopped fresh herbs like

basil, oregano, thyme, rosemary, and parsley)

1 teaspoon garlic

8 ounces baby carrots

1½ pounds quartered baby red potatoes

1. Preheat oven to 425 degrees F. Line a baking sheet with aluminum foil.

2. In a large bowl, toss together olive oil, salt, pepper, Italian seasoning, and garlic. Add carrots and potatoes and toss to combine.

3. Spread potatoes and carrots evenly on pan and bake for 30 minutes.

Nutrition

Calories: 300   Fat: 13g

Carbs: 23g   Fiber: 2g

Sugars: 14g   Protein: 23g

Add-On Options

• ½ cup cooked brown rice: 110 calories

Cooking Tip

Try partially freezing the steak to help make slicing it easier.

Shopping Tip

Pear juice can be a little tricky to find, so check the baby food section of the store. One small bottle is usually exactly the amount you need!

Rollover Ingredients

fresh ginger, green onions

STEAK AND GREEN BEAN STIR-FRY

MAKES 8 (1¼-CUP) SERVINGS

Tender slices of flank steak and crisp green beans are stir-fried with a sweet and savory sauce. To reduce prep right before dinnertime, try slicing the steak, chopping vegetables, and assembling the sauce earlier in the day.

SAUCE

½ cup pear juice (reserve 2 tablespoons)

½ cup soy sauce

⅓ cup brown sugar

1 teaspoon Sriracha sauce

1 teaspoon sesame oil

STEAK

1½ pounds flank steak, trimmed of excess fat

3 tablespoons cornstarch, divided

1–2 tablespoons peanut oil

1 pound green beans

5–7 green onions, chopped (reserve green ends for a flavorful garnish)

1 red, orange, or yellow bell pepper, sliced

3 cloves garlic, minced

1 teaspoon minced fresh ginger

1. Whisk together sauce ingredients, with the exception of the reserved pear juice, and set aside.

2. Slice steak into ¼-inch slices. Sprinkle steak lightly with 1 tablespoon of cornstarch and toss to coat the steak.

3. In a large skillet, heat oil over medium-high heat. Cover bottom of pan with a single layer of steak. Cook 3–5 minutes or until the steak is slightly pink inside. Transfer meat to a plate.

4. Add the green beans to the skillet and cook 2–3 minutes or until they become tender-crisp. Add chopped white ends of the green onions and bell pepper. Cook 1–2 minutes. Add garlic and ginger and cook until fragrant. Return steak to pan and cook until steak is heated through.

5. Turn heat to high and add reserved sauce ingredients. While sauce is heating, whisk together remaining 2 tablespoons cornstarch and reserved pear juice. When sauce is boiling, add cornstarch mixture and cook about 1 minute or until sauce is clear and thickened.

6. Remove from heat and serve immediately over ½ cup hot brown rice.

Nutrition

Calories: 188   **Fat:** 5g

Carbs: 14g   **Fiber:** 8g

Sugars: 5g   **Protein:** 20g

Add-On Options

• 2 small wedges cantaloupe:
  40 calories

Rollover Ingredients

cilantro, fresh ginger, green onions,
lime

Author's Note

This recipe might look intimidating,
but with a little planning, it comes
together easily and is so delicious and
healthy that it's worth it! You can
marinate the pork the night before
and slice the vegetables up to a day
or two ahead of time.—*Kate*

BANH MI TACOS

MAKES 6 SERVINGS

This recipe has a little bit of everything: sweet, spicy, smoky grilled pork is topped with tangy, quick-pickled vegetables and a touch of chili-lime mayonnaise. Best of all, the tacos taste so amazing that you'll never miss the extra calories!

PORK TENDERLOIN MARINADE

1½ pounds pork tenderloin

½ cup soy sauce

¼ cup freshly squeezed lime juice

¼ cup honey

½ teaspoon minced fresh ginger

1½ teaspoons minced garlic

3 green onions, chopped

1 teaspoon Sriracha sauce

2 tablespoons extra-virgin olive oil (basil-flavored oil is also delicious)

1 tablespoon rice vinegar

PICKLED VEGETABLES

1 cup thinly sliced radishes

1 cup carrot shreds

2 cups peeled, sliced cucumbers

1 jalapeño pepper (remove the seeds and white membranes for milder flavor)

1 small red onion, halved and sliced

1 cup rice vinegar

½ cup warm water

½ cup sugar

1 teaspoon kosher salt

Black pepper, to taste

SPICY MAYONNAISE

½ cup light mayonnaise

1 teaspoon freshly squeezed lime juice

1 teaspoon Sriracha sauce

½ teaspoon garlic

HERB MIX

½ cup chopped cilantro

½ cup fresh chopped mint

4 green onions, chopped

6 (6-inch) whole wheat tortillas

1. Place pork tenderloin in a large zip-top bag. Add marinade ingredients to a microwave-safe measuring cup and heat 30 seconds. Whisk together and reserve ¼ cup of marinade. Pour remaining marinade over pork tenderloin, seal the bag, and refrigerate for at least 4 hours.

2. About an hour before serving, toss the vegetables in a medium bowl. Whisk together vinegar, water, sugar, and salt until salt and sugar are dissolved, then pour over vegetables. Season to taste with black pepper and refrigerate until ready to serve.

3. Preheat an outdoor grill to high heat. While grill is heating, whisk together spicy mayonnaise ingredients and place in a squeeze container or a small zip-top bag. Set aside.

4. Toss together the herb mix and set aside.

5. When the grill is hot, place the pork tenderloin on the grill and close the lid. Cook for 7 minutes. Flip the tenderloin and cook for 6 minutes. Leave the lid closed and turn off the heat. Allow tenderloin to stand for 5 minutes. The tenderloin should measure about 155 degrees F. internally.

6. Remove pork from grill, place on a plate or plastic cutting board and lightly cover with a sheet of aluminum foil. Allow tenderloin to rest 3–4 minutes.

7. To serve, slice tenderloin into ¼-inch slices against the grain. Drizzle the reserved marinade over sliced pork. Place 2 ounces of pork in each whole wheat tortilla, then top with pickled vegetables. Cut the corner off the zip-top bag of spicy mayonnaise and squeeze about ½ tablespoon onto the taco.

8. Top with herb mixture and serve immediately.

Nutrition

Calories: 267   Fat: 15g

Carbs: 8g   Fiber: 1g

Sugars: 6g   Protein: 26g

Add-On Options

• *Coconut Rice*

Place 1¼ cups coconut milk (from a carton), ¾ cup water, ½ teaspoon kosher salt, 1 teaspoon sugar, and ½ teaspoon white vinegar in a medium pot on the stove top. Bring to a boil. Rinse 1 cup rice in cool water and drain. Add rice to pot and reduce heat to a simmer. Cover and cook for 20 minutes or until most of the liquid has been absorbed. Allow to stand 5 minutes. Stir in ¼ cup sliced green onions and add additional kosher salt to taste. Makes 6 (½-cup) servings; 123 calories per serving.

• ¾ cup steamed fresh green beans tossed in ½ teaspoon garlic olive oil and ½ teaspoon soy sauce, with kosher salt and black pepper to taste: 66 calories

Shopping Tip

Ask the store butcher to slice the flanken-style ribs fresh for you.

Rollover Ingredient

fresh ginger

HAWAIIAN STYLE RIBS WITH GRILLED PINEAPPLE

MAKES 5–6 SERVINGS; SERVING SIZE IS 2 RIBS PLUS 1 SLICE PINEAPPLE

These sweet, savory ribs bring the tropical flavors of the islands right into your kitchen. Flanken-cut ribs are thin, so they cook up incredibly fast.

2 ½ pounds flanken-cut ribs (about 10–12 ribs)

1½ cups pineapple juice

2 tablespoons brown sugar

1 teaspoon sesame oil

4 tablespoons low-sodium soy sauce

1 tablespoon rice vinegar

2 tablespoons minced fresh ginger

4–5 garlic cloves, minced or pressed

3 green onions, thinly sliced

1 whole pineapple, peeled and sliced into ½-inch slices (about 10–12 slices)

Kosher salt

Black pepper

1. Place ribs in a zip-top bag and set aside.

2. Combine pineapple juice, brown sugar, sesame oil, soy sauce, vinegar, ginger, garlic, and green onions in a bowl and whisk to combine. Pour mixture over ribs in bag and marinate at least 6–8 hours or overnight in the refrigerator. Turn bag occasionally to distribute marinade evenly.

3. Preheat barbecue grill to medium-high heat. Lightly spray pineapple with nonstick cooking spray and sprinkle very lightly with kosher salt. Place ribs and pineapple on grill. (If you have an upper rack on your grill, place pineapple there.) Sprinkle top side of ribs lightly with kosher salt and black pepper.

4. Cook ribs 3–5 minutes on each side until charred and evenly done. Cooking time will depend on thickness of cut. Extra-thin ribs cook for only a couple of minutes per side and thicker cuts (up to ½-inch) may take 5–6 minutes per side. Flip pineapple after a few minutes until it's slightly tender and has grill marks on both sides. Remove both from grill. Serve immediately.

Nutrition

Calories: 136 **Fat:** 4g

Carbs: 18g **Fiber:** 1g

Sugars: 5g **Protein:** 10g

(4 ounces pork alone)

Calories: 200 **Fat:** 13g

Carbs: 0g **Fiber:** 0g

Sugars: 0g **Protein:** 19g

Add-On Options

• ½ tablespoon bottled barbecue sauce: check calories on bottle

Serving Suggestions

The pork recipe can be used for tacos and wraps, on Hawaiian Haystacks, in egg rolls or wontons, on a salad, piled on a Panini or grilled pizza, or tossed in your favorite barbecue sauce.

Shopping Tip

If planning on Kalua pork for a main dish, plan for 6–8 ounces of uncooked meat per person. A 3-pound roast will yield about 1½ pounds finished meat for serving.

Rollover Ingredients

mango, red bell pepper

KALUA PORK SLIDERS WITH PINEAPPLE-MANGO SLAW

MAKES 24 SERVINGS

These bite-sized buns are filled with smoky pork and a bright fresh slaw, shining with tropical flavor. The pork alone is one of our all-time favorite recipes, and a meal-time powerhouse in our own homes. See the many ways we use this easy and delicious pork in the Serving Suggestions tip.

PORK

3 pounds boneless pork shoulder roast

¾ teaspoons kosher salt

2 teaspoons liquid smoke

SLAW

2 cups shredded purple cabbage (cut shreds into about 1-inch pieces)

½ red bell pepper, finely diced

1 rib celery

1/3 cup sliced green onions

3 heaping tablespoons chopped cilantro

½ cup diced mango

½ cup diced pineapple

DRESSING

3 tablespoons light mayonnaise

1 tablespoon cider vinegar

1 teaspoon Dijon mustard

½ teaspoon celery seed

1 tablespoon honey

1 heaping teaspoon orange zest

¼ teaspoon kosher salt

⅛ teaspoon black pepper

¼ teaspoon onion powder

24 Hawaiian sweet rolls

1. Rinse pork roast and pat dry. Pierce entire roast with a fork. Drizzle liquid smoke over roast and rub in on all sides. Sprinkle salt all over roast. Place roast in a slow cooker and cook on low 8–10 hours or until the meat shreds easily with a fork.

2. Remove roast from slow cooker and place on cutting board. Pour out all juices into a fat separator or a glass measuring cup. Shred meat with two forks and discard any extra fat. Return

meat to slow cooker. Skim fat off settled liquid and pour remaining juices back onto pork until moistened and flavored as desired.

3. About 15 minutes before pork is finished, mix slaw ingredients in a large bowl.

4. Whisk dressing ingredients together in a small bowl and then pour over slaw. Toss to combine. Chill in refrigerator until ready to use.

5. To serve, cut rolls in half and top with 1 ounce (about 2 tablespoons) pork and 2 tablespoons slaw mixture.

Nutrition

(2 tacos on corn tortillas with 1½ ounce pork and ¼ cup slaw on each)

Calories: 302   Fat: 8g

Carbs: 32g   Fiber: 5g

Sugars: 8g   Protein: 26g

Add-On Options

• 1 tablespoon light sour cream: 20 calories

• 2 (¼-inch) slices avocado: 50 calories

Alternatives

This same recipe would be delicious with chicken thighs in place of pork. Feel free to replace the corn tortillas with flour or whole-grain, or skip the tortilla and eat as salad instead.

Shopping Tip

Keep an eye out for tortillas that are a blend of both flour and corn. They often provide the flavor of corn tortillas with the softness of flour, for a reasonable amount of calories.

Rollover Ingredient

lime

SMOKY CITRUS PORK TACOS WITH APPLE-CABBAGE SLAW

MAKES 6 SERVINGS; SERVING SIZE IS 2 TACOS

Bright, crunchy slaw complements lean, smoky pork tenderloin in this fun twist on traditional soft tacos.

3–3½ pound pork sirloin roast

1 medium lime, divided

1 medium orange

2 teaspoons minced garlic

½ teaspoon kosher salt

¼ teaspoon freshly ground black pepper

1 tablespoon extra-virgin olive oil

1½ teaspoons liquid smoke

CABBAGE APPLE SLAW

2 cups thinly shredded cabbage

1 cup matchstick-size apple slices

½ cup diced or thinly sliced red onion

½ cup chopped cilantro

1 tablespoon freshly squeezed lime juice

1 tablespoon honey

2 teaspoons olive oil

½ teaspoon kosher salt

4–5 cracks freshly ground black pepper

12 (6-inch) corn or corn-wheat blend tortillas, warmed, or toasted in a skillet

12 thin slices avocado, optional

1.   Rinse pork with cool water and pat dry. Set aside.

2.   To prepare pork, zest both lime and orange into a small bowl. Add minced garlic, kosher salt, black pepper, olive oil, and liquid smoke. Stir to combine. Set bowl aside.

3.   Cut zested orange in half and squeeze juice into a slow cooker. Cut zested lime in half and squeeze half of the lime into the slow cooker (about 1 tablespoon). Reserve other half of lime for slaw. Place pork in slow cooker and turn to coat in citrus juice mix. Pour the citrus zest mixture onto meat and use clean hands to rub all over, coating all sides of meat. Cook on low 6–8 hours.

4.   About 15–20 minutes before pork is finished cooking, combine all slaw ingredients, including reserved lime juice, in large bowl and toss to coat. Refrigerate until ready to use.

5.   Shred pork with two forks and toss with juices in slow cooker. Add additional salt to taste, if needed. Serve pork on tortillas with slaw and avocado, if desired.

Nutrition

Calories: 177   **Fat:** 6g

Carbs: 10g   **Fiber:** 2g

Sugars: 10g   **Protein:** 24g

Add-On Options

- ½ cup cooked brown rice: 110 calories
- 1 cup steamed broccoli: 30 calories

Alternatives

Feel free to replace peaches with another stone fruit of your choice, like nectarines. Fresh mango would also be delicious.

SWEET AND TANGY PORK CHOPS WITH PEACH SALSA

MAKES 4 SERVINGS; SERVING SIZE IS 1 CHOP WITH ½ CUP SALSA

Lean pork chops get a hint of both sweet and tangy with a simple dry rub and fresh peach salsa. With this quick-fix recipe, dinner can be on the table in fewer than 30 minutes!

4 (4-ounce) boneless center cut pork loin chops, about ½-inch thick

1 teaspoon extra-virgin olive oil

1 teaspoon kosher salt

¼ teaspoon freshly ground black pepper

½ teaspoon smoked paprika

½ teaspoon garlic powder

½ teaspoon onion powder

¼ teaspoon chipotle chili powder

PEACH SALSA

2 ripe but slightly firm peaches, diced (about 1 cup)

½ cup diced red bell pepper

⅓ cup diced red onion

½ tablespoon fresh thyme leaves

1 teaspoon honey

1 tablespoon cider vinegar

⅛ teaspoon kosher salt

⅛ teaspoon chili flakes, optional

1. Rinse pork chops with cool water and pat dry with paper towels. Drizzle with olive oil and with clean hands lightly rub in both sides. Combine salt, pepper, smoked paprika, garlic powder, onion powder, and chipotle chili powder in a small bowl. Sprinkle over both sides of all pork chops.

2. Heat outdoor grill, or indoor grill pan, to medium high heat. Cook pork for about 3 minutes on one side, flip, and then continue cooking until internal temperature reaches 150 degrees F.

3. While pork is cooking, combine all salsa ingredients and place in refrigerator until ready to use. Serve each pork chop topped with salsa.

Nutrition

(per 2 crab cakes and 1 generous tablespoon remoulade)

Calories: 234   **Fat:** 12g

Carbs: 13g   **Fiber:** 1g

Sugars: 1g   **Protein:** 19g

Add-On Options

• 4 ounces steamed asparagus drizzled in 1 teaspoon melted salted butter and ½ teaspoon lemon juice: 59 calories

Shopping Tip

Creole mustard is a delicious, mild brown mustard, but it can be a little tricky to find. Try looking for Zatarain's, which is a national brand. If you can't find it, use your favorite mild coarse mustard or omit it entirely.

Rollover Ingredient

green onions

CRAB CAKES

MAKES 4 SERVINGS; SERVING SIZE IS 2 CRAB CAKES

Lump crabmeat is expensive just about any way you cut it, so save these elegant crab cakes for a special occasion. For surf and turf, serve one crab cake with a small grilled beef filet and a salad of leafy greens.

REMOULADE

- 2 tablespoons light sour cream
- 2 tablespoons light mayonnaise
- 1 tablespoon minced green onions
- 1 clove garlic, minced
- 1 teaspoon capers, drained and chopped
- ½ teaspoon Creole mustard
- 1 teaspoon lemon juice
- Pinch kosher salt
- 2–3 cracks coarse freshly ground black pepper

CRAB CAKES

- 1 teaspoon Creole mustard or mild coarse grain mustard
- Pinch of ground red pepper
- 2 cloves garlic, minced
- 4 tablespoons finely chopped green onions
- 3 tablespoons light mayonnaise
- 1 teaspoon grated lemon zest
- 1 tablespoon freshly squeezed lemon juice
- ¼ teaspoon freshly ground black pepper
- 1 pound lump crabmeat, shells picked out and removed
- 1 large egg, beaten
- ⅔ cup panko bread crumbs
- 2 tablespoons extra-virgin olive oil, divided

1. Whisk together remoulade ingredients. Cover and refrigerate until ready to serve with crab cakes.

2. In a medium-sized mixing bowl, combine mustard, red pepper, garlic, green onions, mayonnaise, lemon zest, lemon juice, and black pepper. Add crabmeat and egg. Gently combine with your hands, being careful not to overmix.

3. Add bread crumbs and mix until just combined. Gently form ¼ heaping cup mixture into a patty. Place on a plate or plastic cutting board and cover with plastic wrap. Refrigerate for at least 30 minutes and up to 24 hours.

4. When ready to cook, preheat oven to its lowest setting. On the stove top, heat 1 tablespoon extra-virgin olive oil in a large skillet over medium-high heat. When oil is very hot, carefully add 4 of the crab cakes. Cook about 4 minutes or until golden brown. Carefully flip and cook another 4 minutes. Remove from pan and keep warm in the preheated oven. Repeat with the remaining 1 tablespoon of oil and the remaining 4 crab cakes.

Nutrition

(about 3 ounces fish, ⅙ of the chips, and 1 tablespoon tartar sauce)

Calories: 361 **Fat:** 9g
Carbs: 41g **Fiber:** 3g
Sugars: 3g **Protein:** 22g

Alternative

If you're watching your carbs, you can still enjoy the fish, which has only about 10 carbs—just serve it with a side of coleslaw instead of chips!

Rollover Ingredient

sour cream

Author's Note

One of my favorite early memories is eating fish and chips with my mom, just the two of us, at a fishing boat-themed fast-food fish restaurant. I haven't seen one of those chains for years, but if I did, I'd probably pop in for a basket of fish, just to see how it compares to my memory.—*Kate*

CRISPY BAKED FISH AND CHIPS

MAKES 6 SERVINGS

Traditional fish and chips are a beloved splurge, but it's hard to justify them on a regular basis! Until now. Crispy rice cereal helps keep the coating airy and light, and the crispy roasted potatoes are every bit as good as the ones that come from a fryer. Be sure to serve this dish with a bottle of malt vinegar on the table.

CHIPS

2 tablespoons extra-virgin olive oil
2 teaspoons cornstarch
1 teaspoon kosher salt
1 pound russet potatoes, scrubbed

TARTAR SAUCE

¼ cup light mayonnaise
1 tablespoon low-fat sour cream
⅛ teaspoon dried dill
¼ teaspoon dried parsley flakes
1 teaspoon finely minced onion
1½ teaspoons minced dill pickle
Pinch seasoned salt
½–1 teaspoon freshly squeezed lemon juice, to taste

FISH

¼ cup all-purpose flour
¾ teaspoon kosher salt
¼ teaspoon ground black pepper
1 egg, whisked
2 cups crispy rice cereal
20 ounces firm white fish fillets (cod, halibut, or haddock)

1. Preheat oven to 450 degrees F.

2. Line two baking sheets with slightly crumpled aluminum foil. (This will allow the air to circulate under the foil during cooking and help ensure a crispier end product.) Coat sheet with nonstick cooking spray and set aside.

3. In a medium-sized mixing bowl, whisk together olive oil, cornstarch, and salt. Set aside.

4. Cut potatoes horizontally into 5–6 slices and then again vertically, making French fry-shaped pieces of potato. Place potato pieces in olive oil mixture and toss to combine. Place potatoes on one of the prepared baking sheets and place baking sheet on the lower rack of oven. Bake 20 minutes. Remove pan from oven, flip potatoes, then return pan to oven for another 15–25 minutes or until potatoes are crispy and golden brown.

5. While the potatoes are cooking, whisk together tartar sauce ingredients and set aside.

6. About 20 minutes before potatoes are finished baking, prepare batter for fish by whisking together flour, salt, and pepper in a shallow bowl or pie plate. Crack egg in another small bowl and whisk it. In a third shallow bowl or pie plate, place the crispy rice cereal and lightly crush about ⅓ of it with your hands.

7. Working with one piece of fish at a time, coat the fish in the flour mixture. Transfer the fish to your other hand and coat it in the egg, then transfer it to the bowl of cereal and used your first hand to coat the fish in the cereal. (This is so only one hand touches the raw egg).

8. Place fish on the other prepared baking sheet and repeat with the remaining fish. Bake for 12 minutes or until the fish flakes easily with a fork (or an internal temperature reads 155 degrees F.). Serve immediately with tartar sauce, malt vinegar, and chips on the side.

Nutrition

(grilled honey-lime shrimp)

Calories: 200	Fat: 7.6g
Carbs: 8.3g	Fiber: 0g
Sugars: 7g	Protein: 23g

(tropical quinoa salad)

Calories: 136	Fat: 7g
Carbs: 17g	Fiber: 3g
Sugars: 3g	Protein: 2g

Cooking Tip

Metal or wooden skewers are great for keeping the shrimp from falling through the grates of the grill, but threading them can be time consuming. A grilling basket, either reusable or disposable, is a great alternative—just toss the shrimp into the basket and you get all the flavor from cooking the shrimp on the grill without the hassle.

Rollover Ingredient

green onions

GRILLED HONEY-LIME SHRIMP

MAKES 4 (4-OUNCE) SERVINGS

Garlic, lime, and green onions infuse these shrimp with lots of flavor before they're tossed on the grill and caramelized from the honey in the marinade. Serve alone or with the Tropical Quinoa Salad.

½ cup freshly squeezed lime juice

¼ cup extra-virgin olive oil

2 teaspoons minced garlic

¼ cup honey

Zest of 2 limes

3 green onions, chopped and divided (chop two together and keep the other chopped onion separate)

½ teaspoon kosher salt

⅛ teaspoon freshly ground black pepper

1 pound fresh shrimp, shelled and deveined

1. Whisk together all ingredients except reserved green onions and shrimp. Reserve 2 tablespoons of the liquid.

2. Place shrimp in a large zip-top bag and add the honey-lime marinade. Refrigerate for at least 30 minutes and up to 4 hours.

3. Heat grill to medium-high heat. Place a grill basket on the grill and add shrimp. Cook 3–4 minutes per side. Drizzle reserved liquid over shrimp and sprinkle with reserved green onions before serving.

TROPICAL QUINOA SALAD

MAKES 4 SERVINGS

2 cups cooked quinoa

1½ cups diced fresh pineapple

1 large, seeded jalapeño

2 cloves minced garlic

4 chopped green onions

¼ cup freshly squeezed lime juice

1 teaspoon red wine vinegar

2 tablespoons extra-virgin olive oil

½ teaspoon kosher salt

¼ teaspoon freshly ground black pepper

1 diced avocado

1. In a medium bowl, combine quinoa, pineapple, jalapeño, garlic, and green onions.

2. In a small bowl, whisk together lime juice, red wine vinegar, olive oil, kosher salt, and black pepper. Drizzle over the quinoa mixture. Add avocado and toss gently.

Nutrition

Calories: 345 **Fat:** 20g

Carbs: 10g **Fiber:** 0g

Sugars: 0g **Protein:** 30g

Add-On Options

- Side salad, see page 30
- 4 ounces steamed asparagus drizzled in 1 teaspoon melted salted butter and ½ teaspoon lemon juice: 59 calories

Cooking Tips

- Grate your own cheese for this recipe. Pre-shredded cheese packages are convenient, but the cheese is drier and is coated in a powder that keeps it from sticking, resulting in cheese that doesn't melt very well.
- These can also be made in individual gratin dishes, which is great for portion control and definitely makes this meal feel fancy. Just spray individual gratin dishes with nonstick cooking spray, then divide the fish, sauce, cheese, and bread crumbs evenly between the individual dishes. Place the dishes on a single baking sheet and then place the entire sheet in the oven for the same amount of baking time.

Rollover Ingredient

fresh chives

HALIBUT AU GRATIN

MAKES 6 (⅔-CUP) SERVINGS

If you have non-fish-eaters in your family, this is the recipe for them! Firm white fish is served in a creamy sauce and topped with melted cheddar cheese. You can instantly elevate this to company-worthy status by serving this in individual gratin dishes rather than a pie plate.

½ cup plain panko bread crumbs

1½ teaspoons extra-virgin olive oil

¼ teaspoon kosher salt

1½ teaspoon minced fresh parsley

1 cup 1% milk

2 tablespoons all-purpose flour

½ teaspoon kosher salt

5–6 cracks freshly ground black pepper

1½ ounces light cream cheese

1½ teaspoons butter

2 cloves garlic, minced

½ cup freshly grated Parmesan cheese

1 pound halibut fillets, patted dry with paper towels

Kosher salt and black pepper, to taste

3 tablespoons minced chives

½ cup shredded medium or sharp cheddar cheese

1. Preheat oven to 375 degrees F. Spray a 9-inch pie plate with nonstick cooking spray.

2. In a medium-sized bowl, mix together bread crumbs, olive oil, salt, and parsley. Set aside.

3. Place milk, flour, salt, black pepper, and light cream cheese in a blender and blend until smooth. Set aside.

4. Melt butter in a medium skillet over medium heat. When butter is melted, add garlic and cook 2–3 minutes or until tender and fragrant.

5. Add milk mixture and cook until it's the consistency of a creamy soup. Remove from heat and add Parmesan cheese. Whisk to combine, and then cover pan and allow it to stand for a few minutes.

6. While the sauce is resting, cut halibut into 1-inch chunks and place it in the prepared pie plate. Season lightly with kosher salt and freshly ground black pepper. Sprinkle with chives.

7. Pour sauce over fish. Sprinkle with shredded cheddar cheese and top with bread crumb mixture. Bake for 18 minutes or until fish flakes easily with a fork or internal temperature reads 145 degrees F. Allow to stand for 5 minutes before serving.

Nutrition

Calories: 335   **Fat:** 25g

Carbs: 0g   **Fiber:** 0g

Sugars: 0g   **Protein:** 26g

Add-On Options

• ½ cup cooked brown rice: 110 calories

• 1 cup steamed broccoli: 30 calories

Cooking Tip

Fish might seem intimidating to cook; there's a pretty short window of time between undercooked and over-cooked, and sometimes the fishy flavor can be overwhelming. That said, fish doesn't have to taste fishy; try to buy fish the same day you plan to use it. And fish cooks very quickly, meaning dinner can be on the table in just a few minutes. Serve with steamed vegetables and heat up a pouch of brown rice or quinoa for a super-quick meal.

Rollover Ingredient

lime

SPICY CITRUS SALMON

MAKES 8 (4-OUNCE) SERVINGS

A whole filet of salmon is rubbed with citrus garlic butter and either roasted or grilled in this deceptively simple, super-elegant dish.

2 pounds salmon filet

¼ teaspoon red pepper flakes

½ teaspoon minced garlic

2 teaspoons orange zest

2 teaspoons lime zest

2 teaspoons lemon zest

4 tablespoons salted butter, softened

Salt and pepper, to taste

1. Brush a lined baking sheet with extra-virgin olive oil. Set aside.

2. Preheat oven to 425 degrees F. When the oven is fully heated, place the pan in the oven to preheat the pan.

3. Rinse fish and pat dry with paper towels. Mix red pepper flakes, garlic, and citrus zest with butter. Reserve 1 tablespoon of the seasoned butter and set aside. Spread remaining butter over the fish and season with salt and pepper.

4. Carefully place fish, skin side down, on the hot baking sheet and cook 14–18 minutes or until the thickest part of the fish flakes easily with a fork and internal temperature measures at least 145 degrees F. Remove from oven and spread reserved butter over fish. Serve immediately.

Grilling Instructions: To grill the salmon, preheat an outdoor grill to medium-high heat. Rinse the filet with cool water and pat dry with paper towels. Reserve 1 tablespoon of the seasoned butter and spread the rest over filet. Brush the grate of the grill with oil and carefully place the fish, skin side down, on the grill. Close the lid and cook 10–15 minutes or until the thickest part of the fish flakes with a fork. Remove from heat, place on a serving platter, and spread with the reserved butter. Serve immediately.

Nutrition

Calories: 236   Fat: 7.3g

Carbs: 33g   Fiber: 6g

Sugars: 4g   Protein: 10g

Add On options

• 1 tablespoon light sour cream: 20 calories

• 2 (¼-inch) slices avocado: 50 calories

Alternatives

If you're making this for kids, or mouths who aren't fond of mild heat, leave out the jalapeño and substitute regular Jack cheese or Colby Jack for the pepper Jack.

Rollover Ingredients

cilantro, lime, mango, red pepper

Author's Note

Black beans and mango will forever be one of my favorite flavor combinations. I love this mix of hot, cheesy quesadillas with cold, fresh salsa. The sweet and savory combination is one of my family's favorites. It's also one of my go-to snacks for parties. Assemble the quesadillas ahead of time and store in fridge. When ready to cook, bake lots at once on cookie sheets in the oven.–Sara

BLACK BEAN AND MANGO QUESADILLAS

MAKES 6 SERVINGS

This quick and easy meatless meal is simple to prepare and full of flavor. With a nice amount of both protein and fiber, it will fill you up for a quick weeknight meal or provide a hearty appetizer for your next party.

MANGO SALSA

¾ cup diced mango

3 tablespoons diced red onion

¼ cup diced red bell pepper

1 tablespoon finely minced jalapeño pepper

2 tablespoons chopped cilantro

1–2 tablespoons freshly squeezed lime juice

Salt and pepper, to taste

BLACK BEANS

1 can black beans, drained and rinsed

¼ teaspoon ground cumin

¼ teaspoon coriander

¼ teaspoon onion powder

¼ teaspoon garlic powder

2 tablespoons water

¼ teaspoon kosher salt, divided

Freshly ground black pepper

6 (6–8-inch) flour tortillas

¾ cup shredded pepper Jack cheese

1. Set out a large griddle or skillet, or preheat oven to 400 degrees F. (See cooking method options on page 119.)

2. To prepare mango salsa, combine mango, red onion, bell pepper, jalapeño, cilantro, and lime juice in a bowl. Add ⅛ teaspoon salt and a few cracks of pepper. Gently stir to combine and place in refrigerator to chill.

3. Place beans, cumin, coriander, onion powder, garlic powder, water, ⅛ teaspoon kosher salt, and a few cracks of black pepper in a microwave-safe bowl and stir. Cover with plastic wrap and prick plastic with a fork to vent. Microwave for about 1½ minutes (microwave times vary) until beans are hot. Use a fork to lightly mash beans, leaving some beans still intact.

4. Divide bean mixture between 6 tortillas (2–3 tablespoons each) and spread to cover half of each tortilla. Top each tortilla with 2 tablespoons cheese and fold in half to close. Lightly spray both sides of tortillas with nonstick cooking spray and cook on stove top or in the oven.

5. Let cooked quesadillas rest 3–4 minutes and then carefully open. Add 3 tablespoons mango salsa to each quesadilla and close again.

Stove Top Cooking: Heat a griddle or large skillet to medium high heat. Place quesadillas on warm pan, in batches if necessary, and cook on both sides until toasted and golden and cheese is melted.

Oven Cooking: Place quesadillas in a single layer on a large rimmed baking sheet. Bake 8–10 minutes, until edges are toasted golden brown and slightly crisp.

Nutrition

Calories: 238 **Fat:** 11g

Carbs: 25g **Fiber:** 1g

Sugars: 3g **Protein:** 9g

Cooking Tip

Fresh mozzarella is incredibly soft and can be hard to slice thinly. Place it in the freezer for a few minutes to help it firm up, or simply tear or crumble it over the top of your pizza instead.

Shopping Tip

Naan, or Indian-style flatbread, is found near the bakery or deli departments of the grocery store. It often comes in packs of two.

Rollover Ingredient

basil

GRILLED VEGETABLE FLATBREAD PIZZA

MAKES 6 SERVINGS

Soft, Indian-style flatbreads make the perfect base for savory grilled vegetables and melted cheese. Pair with a nice salad or fruit dish for a light dinner, or cut into small servings for a great party appetizer.

2 store-bought Naan-style flatbreads, about 8–9 ounces total

Nonstick canola or olive oil cooking spray

1 small to medium zucchini, sliced diagonally in ⅛-inch slices

3 horizontal slices red onion, ¼-inch thick (keep rings intact)

Pinch of kosher salt

Black pepper

4 tablespoons pesto

4 tablespoons part-skim ricotta cheese

½ teaspoon minced garlic

2 teaspoons freshly squeezed lemon juice

2 tomatoes, sliced extra thin

4 ounces fresh mozzarella cheese, sliced extra thin

2–3 tablespoons chopped basil

2 teaspoons balsamic vinegar

1. Preheat oven to 400 degrees F. Place flatbreads on a baking sheet and bake for 8 minutes. Remove from oven.

2. Heat a large indoor grill pan (or outdoor barbecue grill) to medium heat. Lightly spray one side of zucchini and onion rings and sprinkle with salt and pepper. When grill pan is hot, place zucchini and onion, oil-side-down, on grill pan and cook 3–5 minutes or until slightly softened and grill marks appear.

3. Spray remaining side with oil and sprinkle with salt and pepper. Flip vegetables and cook an additional 3–5 minutes. Work in batches if necessary.

4. While vegetables are cooking, combine pesto, ricotta, garlic, and lemon juice in a small bowl. Spread mixture on baked flatbreads. Layer grilled zucchini and onion, along with tomatoes and mozzarella, on the flatbreads.

5. Return flatbreads to oven and bake 10–12 minutes, until edges appear toasted and cheese is melted. Remove from oven, sprinkle with basil and drizzle with balsamic vinegar. Let rest for 5 minutes before slicing.

Nutrition

Calories: 268   **Fat:** 12g

Carbs: 32g   **Fiber:** 7g

Sugars: 6g   **Protein:** 11g

Add-On Options

- 1 cup cubed watermelon: 46 calories
- 1 ounce Kettle-style potato chips (about 13 chips): 150 calories

Rollover Ingredient

fresh rosemary

PORTOBELLO BURGER

MAKES 4 SERVINGS

Whether or not you have vegetarian guests, the next time you have a barbecue, try throwing a few of these mushroom burgers on the grill—this portobello burger is so flavorful that you'll never miss the meat!

GARLIC AIOLI

⅓ cup light mayonnaise

1 teaspoon garlic

1 tablespoon lemon juice

1½ teaspoons minced rosemary

5–6 cracks freshly ground black pepper

PORTOBELLO BURGERS

4 medium portobello mushroom caps, washed and patted dry

8 teaspoons light balsamic vinaigrette

4 whole wheat hamburger buns

4 thin slices smoked provolone cheese

1 avocado, quartered and cut into slices

4 lettuce leaves

10–12 thin slices red onion

1. Whisk together garlic aioli ingredients in a small bowl and set aside.

2. Preheat outdoor grill to medium-high heat.

3. Brush each mushroom cap on both sides with 2 teaspoons balsamic vinaigrette. Place mushroom caps on heated grill and cook for about 7 minutes per side.

4. During the last 1–2 minutes of cooking, place the buns face down on the grill and top each mushroom cap with a slice of cheese. Close the lid for an additional 1–2 minutes or until bread is toasted and cheese is melted. Remove everything from grill.

5. Spread each side of the bun with 1 teaspoon of garlic aioli. Top with a leaf of lettuce, onion slice, cooked mushroom cap, and ¼ sliced avocado per burger. Serve immediately.

Nutrition

Calories: 309   **Fat:** 16g

Carbs: 32g   **Fiber:** 7g

Sugars: 3g   **Protein:** 12g

Add-On Options

• 1 cup fresh strawberries: 53 calories

• ½ navel orange: 40 calories

Alternatives

If you'd rather leave out the tortilla, increase spinach to 5 cups and serve as a salad.

Rollover Ingredient

feta cheese

VEGGIE, HUMMUS, AND FETA WRAP

MAKES 1 SERVING

Whether you work in an office or at home, making a healthy grown-up lunch for one person can be a hard challenge. This meatless wrap is hearty and satisfying, but packed with vegetables and healthy fats to keep you going all afternoon.

2 tablespoons roasted red pepper hummus

1 (10-inch) whole wheat tortilla

1–1½ cups fresh spinach

½ cup chopped cucumber or 1 baby English cucumber, sliced

2–3 tablespoons chopped roasted red pepper

2 tablespoons crumbled low-fat feta cheese

1 tablespoon sunflower seeds

1 tablespoon low-fat Italian salad dressing

Spread the hummus on the tortilla. Layer the remaining ingredients, drizzling with the dressing last. Wrap and eat immediately.

Nutrition

Calories: 160 **Fat:** 3g

Carbs: 26g **Fiber:** 2g

Sugars: 8g **Protein:** 3g

ANGEL FOOD STACKS WITH LEMON CREAM AND FRESH BERRIES

MAKES 8 (½-INCH SLICE) SERVINGS

Light and airy angel food cake is the perfect base for luscious lemony cream and honey-kissed berries. You could also layer the ingredients into small jars or bowls for a trifle-style dessert.

2 ounces reduced-fat cream cheese, at room temperature

4 tablespoons lemon curd

1 cup frozen whipped topping, thawed

2 cups mixed fresh berries (raspberries, blueberries, sliced strawberries)

1 teaspoon freshly squeezed lemon juice

1 teaspoon honey

2 teaspoons finely minced fresh mint, optional

8 (1-ounce) slices angel food cake

1. Beat cream cheese and lemon curd in a small mixing bowl until smooth and creamy. Gently fold in whipped topping using a rubber spatula until combined. (Do not beat.)

2. In a separate bowl, combine berries, lemon juice, honey, and mint, and gently toss to combine.

3. To assemble, cut each slice of angel food cake in half. Spread 1 rounded tablespoon lemon cream on one half of cake and top with the other half. Top with an additional rounded tablespoon of lemon cream and then cover with about ¼ cup berry mixture.

Nutrition

Calories: 150   **Fat:** 4g

Carbs: 28g   **Fiber:** 0g

Sugars: 17g   **Protein:** 3g

Serving Suggestion

Crepes can be served warm, cold, or at room temperature. If storing in refrigerator, cool completely and then layer between sheets of waxed paper or parchment in an air-tight container.

Cooking Tip

Even crepe-cooking experts find that the first one is sometimes a flop! This recipe specifically yields enough batter for 9 crepes, giving you 1 "practice" crepe to start, just in case it's not your prettiest.

CHOCOLATE CREPES WITH BANANAS AND CARAMEL

MAKES 8 SERVINGS

Sophisticated crepes are actually simple to make! These beauties get a chocolate spin and are dressed up with bananas and caramel for a decadent dessert that's quick enough to make on a weeknight.

½ cup nonfat milk

1 egg

1 tablespoon vegetable oil

½ teaspoon vanilla extract

1½ tablespoons sugar

⅓ cup flour

1½ tablespoons unsweetened cocoa powder

Pinch of salt

4 medium bananas

⅓ cup jarred caramel sauce

Whipped cream

Ground cinnamon

1. Place milk, egg, vegetable oil, vanilla, sugar, flour, cocoa powder, and salt in a blender and blend just until smooth.

2. Heat an 8-inch nonstick skillet to medium heat. Water droplets should sizzle when dropped on it. Lightly coat skillet with nonstick cooking spray. While holding skillet with one hand, immediately pour 2 tablespoons crepe batter while rotating pan so batter distributes evenly over pan in a thin layer.

3. Place pan on heat and cook about 30–45 seconds, until edges of crepe are easily loosened from pan with a rubber spatula. Gently lift crepe from pan with spatula and flip. Cook for an additional 15–20 seconds and then transfer to a plate. Cover with foil to keep warm. Continue with batter until all crepes are made, recoating pan lightly with nonstick cooking spray before each crepe.

4. To assemble, place 4 banana slices (about ½ small banana or 1½ ounces) on one quarter of crepe, in a wedge shape. Drizzle with 1 teaspoon caramel sauce. Fold crepe in half over bananas and then in half again to form a triangle. Top with an additional teaspoon caramel sauce and 2 tablespoons whipped cream. Garnish with a dash of cinnamon.

Nutrition

Calories: 156 Fat: 10g

Carbs: 18g Fiber: 4g

Sugars: 5g Protein: 3g

CHOCOLATE PEANUT BUTTER APPLES WITH COCONUT AND ALMONDS

MAKES 2 SERVINGS

Sweet, crisp apples are elevated to dessert level when drizzled with dark chocolate and peanut butter. Crunchy almonds and coconut flakes add flavor and texture, plus a healthy boost of both fiber and protein. This family favorite makes a great after-school snack, too!

1 medium crisp sweet apple

1 tablespoon chopped dark chocolate or chocolate chips

¼ teaspoon coconut or canola oil

1 tablespoon high quality peanut butter, or other nut butter of your choice

1 tablespoon toasted sweetened coconut flakes

½ tablespoon sliced toasted almonds

1. Core apple and slice into ¼-inch slices. Arrange on a plate.

2. Place chocolate and oil in a small bowl and microwave until melted and smooth. In a separate bowl, melt peanut butter 15–20 seconds, until soft and you're able to drizzle it with a spoon.

3. Drizzle chocolate and peanut butter over apples. Sprinkle with coconut and almonds.

Nutrition

(plain cheesecake)

Calories: 122   **Fat:** 7g

Carbs: 11g   **Fiber:** 0g

Sugars: 8g   **Protein:** 5g

Cooking Tip

For extra coconut flavor, add 1½ teaspoons coconut extract to cheesecake batter before baking.

Author's Note

Mini cheesecakes are one of my go-to dishes for entertaining. They're perfectly portioned, and I make them ahead of time so it's one less thing to worry about when entertaining!—*Sara*

MINI CHEESECAKES

MAKES 12 SERVINGS

These perfectly portioned cheesecakes are rich and dreamy, but the individual sizes keep calories in check. They even boast 5 grams of protein per serving. Try them with one of our topping suggestions or invent your own!

CRUST

3 whole graham crackers

1 teaspoon brown sugar

1 dash cinnamon

1½ tablespoons butter, melted

CHEESECAKE

8 ounces reduced-calorie cream cheese (not non-fat)

⅓ cup sugar

1 egg

1 egg white

1 cup 2% cottage cheese

1 teaspoon vanilla extract

1½ tablespoons flour

1. Preheat oven to 350 degrees F. Line a 12-cup muffin tin with foil cupcake liners.

2. To make crust, break graham crackers into food processor and process into fine crumbs (you should have about a scant ½ cup crumbs). Add brown sugar and cinnamon, and pulse to combine. With processor running, drizzle in butter, and process until combined.

3. Divide crust into muffin cups and gently press down with fingers. Bake for 5 minutes and then remove pan from oven.

4. To make cheesecake, beat cream cheese and sugar until smooth. Add egg and egg white and blend until smooth. Place cottage cheese in a food processor and process until smooth and creamy. Add cottage cheese mixture to cream cheese mixture. Add vanilla and flour and beat just until combined, scraping down sides of bowl as necessary.

5. Divide mixture evenly between muffin cups, about ¼ cup in each. Cups will be full. Bake 15–20 minutes, until centers are puffed and edges are set. Remove from oven and cool completely to room temperature. Centers will sink when cooled. Refrigerate for a minimum of 6–8 hours, or overnight. Serve with desired toppings.

Additional Nutrition Per Cheesecake

(berries and cream topping)

Calories: 15	Fat: 1g
Carbs: 3g	Fiber: 0g
Sugars: 2g	Protein: 0g

(apple-cinnamon topping)

Calories: 39	Fat: 2g
Carbs: 5g	Fiber: 0g
Sugars: 4g	Protein: 0g

BERRIES AND CREAM TOPPING

Top each cheesecake with 1 tablespoon whipped cream and 1 tablespoon fresh mixed berries (blueberries, blackberries, raspberries, or chopped strawberries). Garnish with fresh mint.

APPLE-CINNAMON TOPPING

1½ cups diced peeled apple

1 tablespoon brown sugar

¼ teaspoon cinnamon

Dash nutmeg

Whipped cream

¼ cup pure maple syrup

Toasted pecan halves

In a small nonstick sauté pan, combine apple, brown sugar, cinnamon, and nutmeg. Cook on medium heat 5–7 minutes, or until apples are crisp-tender. If apples begin to stick to pan, add

up to 1 tablespoon water. Let cool. Divide apples between cheesecakes, top each with 1 tablespoon whipped cream, drizzle with ¼ teaspoon syrup, and top with a toasted pecan half. Garnish with ground cinnamon if desired.

TROPICAL COCONUT CARAMEL TOPPING

1 cup diced mango

½ teaspoon honey

1 teaspoon freshly squeezed lime juice

½ teaspoon finely grated lime zest

¼ cup toasted coconut

¼ cup caramel sauce

In a small bowl, toss mango with honey, lime juice, and lime zest. Divide between cheesecakes and top each with ¼ teaspoon toasted coconut and ¼ teaspoon caramel sauce.

Nutrition

Calories: 115   **Fat:** 6g

Carbs: 14g   **Fiber:** 1g

Sugars: 11g   **Protein:** 3g

Cooking Tip

Avoid natural-style peanut butter for this recipe. These cookies have best results with regular creamy peanut butter. Also, if using a larger egg, whisk egg white and measure out 2 tablespoons for this recipe; discard the rest.

Shopping Tip

Aim for a slow-churned ice cream around 100 calories per serving. You could also use vanilla frozen yogurt.

PB & J ICE CREAM COOKIE SANDWICHES

MAKES 12 SERVINGS

These darling treats have all of your favorite flavors in one cool, frosty bite. Our soft-baked flourless cookies require only four ingredients, and they're sandwiched with creamy vanilla ice cream and a sweet burst of fruit. Don't be fooled by the small size; these little morsels are huge on taste!

½ cup creamy peanut butter

6 tablespoons packed brown sugar

½ teaspoon baking soda

1 egg white (from medium or large egg, avoid extra large)

1 cup plus 2 tablespoons slow-churned style vanilla ice cream, slightly softened

2 tablespoons raspberry or strawberry preserves

1. Preheat oven to 350 degrees F. Line a baking sheet with parchment paper or a silicone baking mat.

2. Beat peanut butter, brown sugar, baking soda, and egg white until combined. Dough will be loose. Chill for 1 hour in refrigerator. Dough will be soft.

3. Scoop dough by scant ½ tablespoons and gently form into balls. Place on cookie sheet and flatten just slightly with your hand. You should have about 2 dozen cookies.

4. Bake 5–7 minutes, until cookies are puffed and edges are set. Let cool 2–3 minutes on baking sheet and then transfer to cooling rack. Once completely cooled, store in freezer until ready to assemble.

5. To assemble, flip all cookies over and spoon ¼ teaspoon jam on each one. Place 1½ tablespoons vanilla ice cream (a spring-loaded cookie scoop works perfectly) on 12 of the cookies. Sandwich another cookie on top of each of the 12 ice cream-topped cookies, gently pressing them together.

6. Place sandwiches on a plate or freezer-safe container and freeze until firm. To serve, let sit at room temperature for a few minutes to soften.

CATEGORY INDEX

ROLLOVER INGREDIENTS

WE'VE CREATED THIS INDEX TO HELP YOU PLAN MEALS AND USE UP PERISHABLE OR UNCOMMON INGREDIENTS.

INDEX

REFERENCES TO PHOTOGRAPHS ARE IN **BOLD**. RECIPES FOUND IN SIDE BARS ARE IN *ITALICS*.

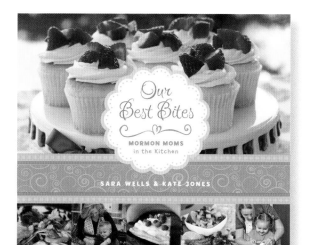

You know you want to try "olive" us!